# NARROW HOUSES

# NARROW HOUSES

## New Directions in Efficient Design

**Avi Friedman**

Princeton Architectural Press, New York

Published by
Princeton Architectural Press
37 East Seventh Street
New York, New York 10003

For a free catalog of books, call 1-800-722-6657
Visit our website at www.papress.com

© 2010 Princeton Architectural Press
All rights reserved
Printed and bound in China
13 12 11 10  4 3 2 1  First edition

Editor: Laurie Manfra
Designer: Paul Wagner

Special thanks to: Nettie Aljian, Sara Bader, Nicola Bednarek,
Janet Behning, Becca Casbon, Carina Cha, Tom Cho,
Penny (Yuen Pik) Chu, Russell Fernandez, Pete Fitzpatrick,
Linda Lee, John Myers, Katharine Myers, Steve Royal, Dan Simon,
Andrew Stepanian, Jennifer Thompson, Joseph Weston,
and Deb Wood of Princeton Architectural Press
—Kevin C. Lippert, publisher

Front cover: photograph by Greg Richardson, © MacKay-Lyons
Sweetapple Architects Limited
Back cover: top photograph courtesy Bearth & Deplazes Architekten,
bottom photograph by Paul Warchol

Library of Congress Cataloging-in-Publication Data
Friedman, Avi, 1952–
Narrow houses : new directions on efficient design /
Avi Friedman. — 1st ed.
    p.   cm.
Includes bibliographical references and index.
ISBN 978-1-56898-873-3 (alk. paper)
1. Small houses. 2. Row houses. 3. Shotgun houses. 4. Space
(Architecture) I. Title.
NA7533.F75 2010
728—dc22
                                    2010018236

# CONTENTS

Many contributed to the preparation of this book. A special thanks in a collection of such a nature needs to be given to the firms who made their material available and to those who participated in its compiling and mailing. Others generously participated in finding the projects: Yixiong Rang, Jeanne Cayer-Desrosier, and Courtney Posel. Natalie Dubois and Bori Yoon helped in background research for the "Design Principles" and "Historical Chronology" essays. Rainier Silva produced the images. Cynthia Nei offered editorial comments. Nyd Garavito-Bruhn prepared the text and formatted the images for publication. They all labored with dedication and care.

To Nancy Eklund Later, a senior acquisitions editor at Princeton Architectural Press, who took part in the project's gestation. To Laurie Manfra, the principal editor, for her much-admired dedication, patience, and effort to make the book complete. To Paul Wagner, for attention to details and creative thinking in the design of the pages. To the faculty and staff of McGill University School of Architecture for their support.

This vote of thanks will not be complete without acknowledging my family: Paloma, Ben, and especially my wife, Sorel Friedman, PhD, for their support and encouragement.

The design of narrow dwellings has been the subject of my research for several decades. In 1990, along with Witold Rybczynski and Susan Ross, we unveiled the Grow Home on the campus of McGill University in Montreal. This 14-by-36-foot (4.3-by-11-meter) unit became a topic of additional inquiry, including studies of its environmental footprint, modes of prefabrication, use in community design, and variations on interior space.

The term *narrow-front* is typically used to describe dwellings whose street-facing exteriors measure 25 feet (6 meters) or less; they can be constructed in a detached, semidetached, or attached form. Also known as terraced homes, townhouses, or shotgun dwellings, they have been constructed throughout history on several continents and have maintained their appeal by offering privacy and green yards, even in compact configurations. Built in high densities, they help halt urban sprawl, reduce the amount of construction material, and improve energy efficiency once occupied.

Recent societal changes have brought about renewed interest in narrow houses among architects, town planners, and housing officials. This building type, which dates back two millenia, offers relevant solutions to contemporary challenges. Chief among them is the need to adopt sustainable approaches to the planning of neighborhoods and houses. Another trend is society's rapidly changing demographics, with a greater number of individuals, single parents, and childless couples wishing to reside in ground-floor units.

This book strives to offer examples of distinctive dwellings and townhouses as well as present the fundamental principles of narrow house design. Divided into two parts, the first part presents twenty-eight case studies of exemplary narrow houses around the world. These examples have been selected for their unique urban solution, intriguing architectural approach, environmental sensitivity, or imaginative interior. Corresponding text, data, drawings, and photographs offer a comprehensive view of a diverse selection of house designs that are inspiring and will most likely be timeless.

The book's second part consists of four essays, beginning with an overview of narrow house design and its relevance to current times. It focuses on the macro issues affecting design, including siting a house, footprints, spatial arrangements, access, and facades; it then walks the reader through the interior, where movement, space distribution, circulation, privacy, and flexibility are explored. The final essay, an illustrated chronology, traces the historical origins and evolution of the narrow house prototype, beginning in classical Greece, continuing through the Middle Ages, and concluding with the contemporary era.

# DETACHED DWELLINGS

The desire to reduce the footprint of a house on a site endowed with natural features was the primary motive behind many of the projects featured in this section. Other objectives included the need to minimize building costs, accommodate a number of functions in a relatively small space, fill in an urban gap, or simply conceive of a sculptural dwelling. These constraints led to innovative thinking and intriguing designs. Locating and bringing light and views to all rooms, including the house's service core, was another concern. In keeping with current environmental challenges, the architects considered orientation for passive solar gain and minimal disruption to the landscape. For urban projects this challenge often derived from a need to conform to existing bylaws and avoid shadows cast by neighboring homes. Despite their small lot sizes, many of the houses include a rear garden, an oasis of sorts, for occupants to enjoy. Attention to both exterior and interior detailing is visible in all of the dwellings. Architectural details were approached meticulously, and they are reflected in the choice of interior finishes and exterior cladding. The homes featured on the following pages have a timeless quality, and they offer valuable lessons that can be applied to common residences and other architectural projects.

# SLIDING HOUSE

Width: 15 ft.

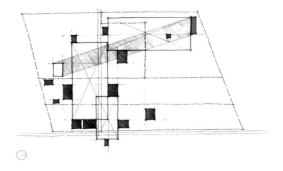

LOCATION
**Upper Kingsburg
Nova Scotia, Canada**

DESIGNER
**MacKay-Lyons Sweetapple
Architects Limited**

COMPLETION
**2008**

SITE AREA
**1.9 acres (0.8 hectare)**

FLOOR AREA
**960 sq. ft. (89 sq. m)**

This house is sited on an agrarian hillside, along a 250-year-old stone wall, with its axis directed eastward down the hill to a lake. In the historic village below, there are three houses belonging to the sons of the original settlers, to which the Sliding House is oriented orthogonally.

The dwelling sets up a tension between a plumb interior and a crooked exterior. A building precedent is the house immediately below, built in 1753, that leans downhill due to 250 years of prevailing westerly winds.

The floor plan addresses a need for refuge. A thick, north-facing service wall containing stairs, baths, kitchen, hearth, and storage protects the house from cold north winds, while the continuous, south-facing ribbon window opens the house to the sun and horizon. The volume of the home pinwheels symmetrically in section toward the horizontal axis of the ribbon window, creating an upper and a lower bedroom.

The rough exterior cladding of industrial corrugated metal is contrasted with a refined interior hardwood liner, completely crafted of bleached, clear poplar. The tilted box allows the roof to drain downhill. The quiet restraint of this aesthetic lets the landscape dominate, with minimal form and maximum content.

above: Site plan
opposite: Living area

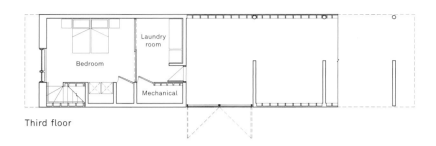

Third floor

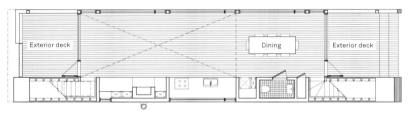

Second floor

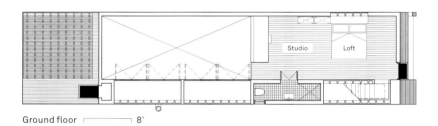

Ground floor ⌐————⌐ 8'

left: Side elevation
middle: Front elevation

right: Rear elevation

Sideways view

Living, kitchen, and dining areas

top: Bedroom
bottom: Dining and living areas

# HOLLY BARN

Width: 20 ft.

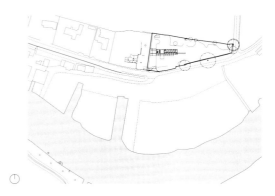

LOCATION
**Reedham**
**Norfolk, England**

DESIGNER
**Knox Bhavan Architects**

COMPLETION
**2005**

SITE AREA
**1.2 acres (0.5 hectare)**

FOOTPRINT
**1,745 sq. ft. (162 sq. m)**

TOTAL FLOOR AREA
**3,014 sq. ft. (280 sq. m)**

The designers of the Holly Barn had the difficult task of building on an environmentally sensitive location at the edge of the Norfolk Broads in the village of Reedham in Norfolk, England. The large edifice, measuring 89 by 20 feet (27 by 6 meters), had its profile softened by smooth curves to allow it to blend smoothly with the skyline.

The house has its primary living spaces and a bedroom suite on the ground floor. This, combined with wide passages and doorways, a platform lift, and handrails, helps the wheelchair-bound owner navigate the house easily. It was not achieved at the expense of visual appeal, however, as wide windows offer excellent views of the surrounding landscape, and the curving ceiling lends a pleasing air to the overall interior.

In all, there are five bedrooms: four on the ground floor and the fifth and largest on the second floor. The ground floor also contains kitchen, dining, and sitting rooms with large windows that offer views from a higher vantage point during mealtimes. In addition, there is a playroom, as well as a communal area, outside the lower four bedrooms.

The designers used natural larch boarding to clad the walls and roof, mimicking the area's more traditional architecture, including local windmills and boathouses.

above: Site plan
opposite: View of gable

Bathroom

Bedroom

Bedroom

Bedroom

Bedroom

Bathroom

Play room

Hall

Lift

Ground floor ⊢————————⊣ 6'

Bedroom

Bathroom

Study

Sitting room

Kitchen

Dining room

Void to hall    Lift

Second floor

top left: Front elevation
top right: Detail of gable window

bottom: Holly Barn at dusk

Detail of stairs

top: Kitchen and dining areas
bottom: Bathroom pod

# BIAGI HOUSE

Width: 13 ft.

LOCATION

**Todds Point
Kentucky, United States**

DESIGNER

**David Biagi**

COMPLETION

**1993**

SITE AREA

**60 acres (24 hectares)**

TOTAL FLOOR AREA

**900 sq. ft. (84 sq. m)**

Kentucky-born architect and professor David Biagi developed his sense of space (or using a minimal amount of it) while working and living in New York City, where he mastered the skills of making small areas feel big. These skills came in handy when, in 1992, he returned to Louisville to join his family's architectural practice and began to design his own home. Budget was a key concern. Naturally, designing a small home would bring the cost down. The two-sided challenge of needing to reduce cost and make a small dwelling feel spacious resulted in a beautifully sculpted home, which has been inserted into an embankment.

Biagi attained a low cost by using standard construction components. The windows, for example, were chosen from a catalog, and the kitchen cabinets were fabricated from plywood, with birch and cherry veneers.

One device Biagi used to great effect in the design was the illusion of distance, which he created by offering a diagonal, rather than horizontal, line of view. This first line of site occurs outside, when approaching the front of the house (situated on a hill). This entrance sequence causes the viewer to look up and across, enhancing the house's perceived size. Once inside, the same method of offering an upward-angled diagonal view comes into play, as the open entrance area, combined with a slanting staircase, allows the visitor to see from one corner of the house to nearly its opposite. Many large windows permit unobstructed site lines past the perimeter of the house, further amplifying the sense of space.

Perspective view

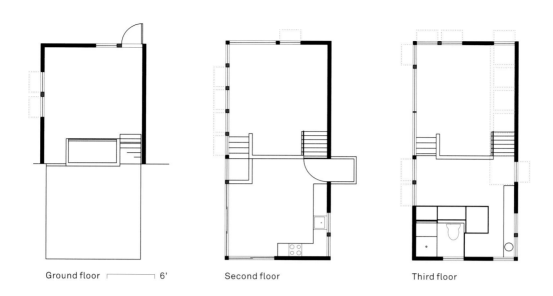

Ground floor ⊢────────⊣ 6'    Second floor    Third floor

left: Interior view
right: Living room corner

top: Interior view
bottom: Living room

# HOUSE MS

Width: 18 ft.

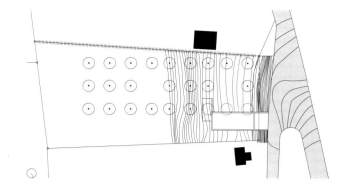

LOCATION
**Huccorgne, Belgium**

DESIGNER
**Martiat Durnez, Architectes**

COMPLETION
**2007**

FOOTPRINT
**738 sq. ft. (68.8 sq. m)**

FLOOR AREA
**1,650 sq. ft. (153 sq. m)**

This dwelling was designed to house a couple and their two children. The need to conserve the site, which is located at the edge of the village of Huccorgne in rural Belgium, dictated the concept. Strict regulations mandated careful attention to the landscape. Siting the house on the property's edge allowed much of the land to remain untouched. The flat roof keeps the profile of the dwelling low. Rather than build above ground, the house is inserted into the terrain, thereby maintaining the existing embankment. The street-facing facade measures only 18 feet (5.5 meters) wide.

The unit's functions were arranged in a reverse order from a typical home. The entrance is at street level, where a play area and mechanical room are housed. The children's bedrooms are on the second floor, with a view to the southwest contributing to passive solar gain. The public functions, as well as the master bedroom, are located on the third floor, along with a cantilevered, enclosed terrace. The cantilever reduces the home's footprint. To make maximum use of interior space, a simple layout was conceived, with the placement of the stair along the longitudinal wall. Large openings at the rear and side let in plenty of natural light, adding to the perception of spaciousness.

The selection of cladding enhances the house's site integration. Untreated vertical red cedar was used on the facades. The window frames, made of Afzelia wood, match the cedar.

above: Site plan
opposite: Detail of facade

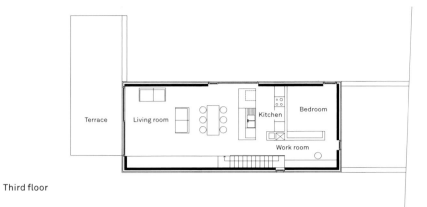

Third floor

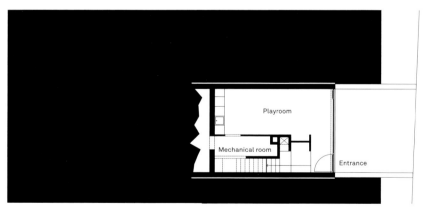

Second floor

Ground floor ⌐————⌐ 9'

top: Rear view

bottom left: View from the road
bottom right: Perspective view

top: Side view
bottom: Upward view

top: Cantilever detail
bottom: Living and dining area

# CHAMELEON HOUSE

Width: 16 ft.

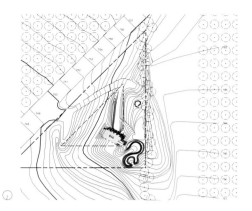

**Northport
Michigan, United States**

DESIGNER

**Anderson Anderson
Architecture**

COMPLETION

**2004**

SITE AREA

**0.7 acre (0.3 hectare)**

FOOTPRINT

**480 sq. ft. (44.6 sq. m)**

FLOOR AREA

**1,476 sq. ft. (137 sq. m)**

Rising above the rolling topography of an orchard, Chameleon House captures spectacular views of Lake Michigan and the surrounding agricultural landscape. With the exception of two mounded enclosures made from earth excavated for the foundation, the site is minimally disturbed. Due to the slope, occupants enter at the third level and descend to the kids' bedrooms or climb up to the main living spaces, which overlook the surrounding cherry orchard.

The house is intended to reflect the austere, scaleless farm buildings that dot the hills. To help mask the scale, the building is wrapped in a skirting wall of recycled translucent polyethylene slats, which stand 2 feet (0.6 meter) out from the galvanized sheet-metal wall cladding, hung on aluminum frames that serve as window washing platforms and emergency exit ladders. The cladding material was chosen for its ability to reflect the light and color of the surrounding landscape, dissolving the shadowed structure into the seasonal color cycle of snow, ice, and black twig tracery in winter; pale pink blossom clouds in spring; pollen, green leaf, and grass in summer; and golden straw and vivid foliage in fall. The double skin creates a microclimate around the structure and an updraft that, in summer, sends steaming condensation upward or, in winter, drips melting icicles.

To keep cost and on-site labor to a minimum, structural insulated panels (SIPs) were used for the exterior walls. By using common materials and industrial detailing, a commercial contractor was able to build the home in less than three months.

above: Site plan
opposite: View of southwest corner

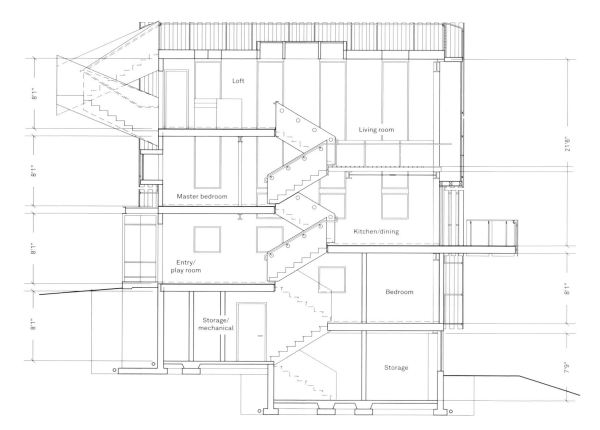

Section

Exterior detail views of reflective acrylic slats and glazing

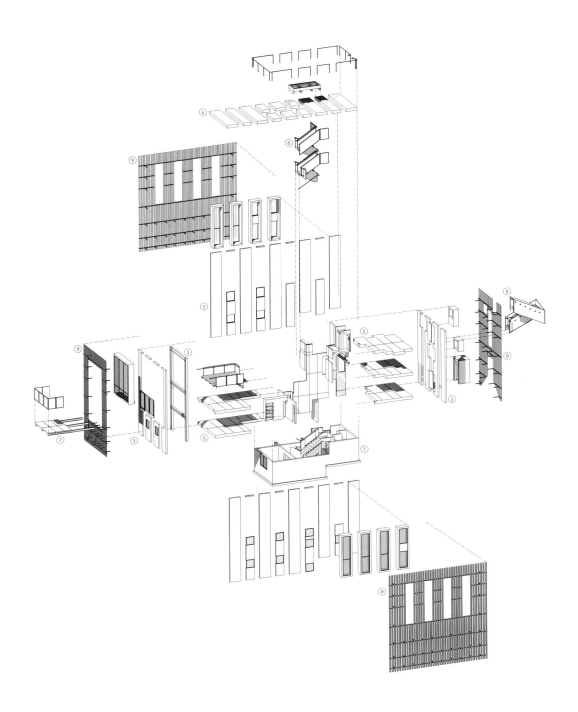

Building parts in order of assembly:
1 Concrete foundation and basement
2 Wide-flange moment frame
3 SIP wall panels and window boxes
4 SIP roof panels
5 Panelized floors
6 Prefabricated steel interior stair and railings
7 Cantilevered terrace
8 Prefabricated steel roof-access stair
9 Acrylic screen with tube-steel frame

Cantilevered roof-access stair

top left: Loft area
top right: Living room

bottom left: Dining area
bottom right: View from dining area

Morning sun reflecting off the northeast facade

# WOHNHAUS WILLIMANN-LÖTSCHER

**Width: 16 ft.**

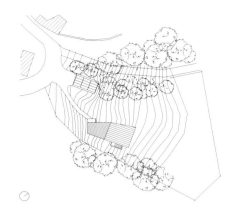

LOCATION
**Sevgein, Switzerland**

DESIGNER
**Bearth & Deplazes Architekten**

COMPLETION
**1999**

FLOOR AREA
**590 sq. ft. (55 sq. m)**

A house with lots of different rooms—a kind of labyrinthine mousehole—was what this family of four wanted. The result is a vertical arrangement of rooms offset at each half-story, following the slope of the site. Situated in a woodland clearing on the edge of a village, the house is wedged between the side of a mountain and the end of a chain of hills, forming a gentle transition between the two. From this position, it offers a view across the Upper Rhine Valley.

One each floor, two rooms are arranged along a long, shared wall to create a spiraling vertical space within the house. This approach maximizes the interior volume despite the small individual room sizes. The entrance to the house opens into a two-story-high hallway, with steps leading down to the dining room and kitchen and up to a living room with gallery. Four more rooms occupy the stories above.

The timber frame was prefabricated in sections, and standard windows were prefitted on the facades and roof. According to the architects, the clients did much of the finishing work themselves, including painting the exterior cladding.

above: Site plan

Front elevation

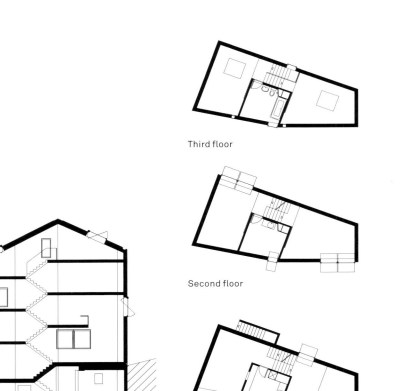

Third floor

Second floor

Ground floor ⊢——————⊣ 12'

Section 1

Section 2

bottom: View of the Upper Rhine Valley

top: Side view
bottom: Rear view

# SALT POINT HOUSE

**Width: 25 ft.**

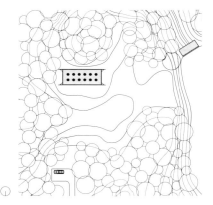

LOCATION
**Salt Point
New York, United States**

DESIGNER
**Thomas Phifer and Partners**

COMPLETION
**2007**

SITE AREA
**7 acres (2.8 hectares)**

FOOTPRINT
**1,125 sq. ft. (104.1 sq. m)**

FLOOR AREA
**1,184 sq. ft. (110 sq. m)**

Constructed of elegantly efficient and economical materials, this 2,200-square-foot (204-square-meter) house in New York's Hudson Valley is sited on a meadow with views to a small private lake.

Relatively solid on the north and south facades, the house opens to the landscape on the east and west. A double-height entry hall on the eastern end, tucked into the surrounding woods, allows an immediate understanding of the home's organization: living spaces downstairs, sleeping and work quarters upstairs.

At the west end, a double-height porch connects the two levels, extending the living area downstairs while allowing views to the lake from the bedrooms.

From the lower level, continuous slot windows, set in the north and south walls, frame distinct views of the surrounding greenery. At the upper level, sculpted skylight enclosures offer glimpses of the changing sky throughout the day and night.

To reduce costs, the house was designed to be compact. Building materials were selected for function, durability, and economy. Interior walls, floors, and ceilings are clad in maple plywood, as well as custom furniture and interior cabinetry. Standard commercial fluorescent light fixtures are recessed into narrow slots in the plywood to provide inexpensive but elegant lighting.

Exterior stainless steel screen panels on the north and south facades are held a few inches off the main structure to protect the house from extreme summer sun and winter winds. The perforated screens shade the exterior, creating a thermal buffer, which helps keep the interior cool. Strategically placed operable windows and ventilating skylights allow breezes to flow through the home. Natural interior ventilation, along with the shading effect of exterior sunscreens, keeps the house comfortably habitable (without air conditioning) throughout the warm summer months.

above: Site plan

Front view

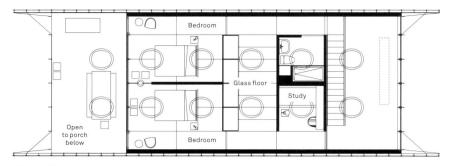

Second floor

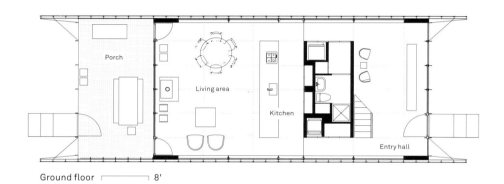

Ground floor ⌐————⌐ 8'

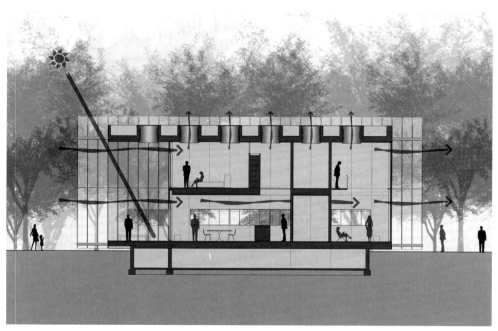

Section

top: Perspective view
bottom: Side elevation

Side view detail

Interior view

# PINE FOREST CABIN

**Width: 16 ft.**

LOCATION
**Methow Valley
Washington, United States**

DESIGNER
**Cutler Anderson Architects**

COMPLETION
**1999**

SITE AREA
**5 acres (2 hectares)**

FOOTPRINT
**672 sq. ft. (63.7 sq. m)**

FLOOR AREA
**1,345 sq. ft. (125 sq. m)**

Pine Forest Cabin was designed to suit its context. The home, which serves as a year-round retreat, is located in a sloping forested area and takes advantage of the trees that cast shadows in summertime and block winds in winter. The exposed solid-sawn pine cladding on the exterior helps integrate the house with the site. The dwelling rests on fourteen pyramid-shaped concrete piers, making it feel as though it's floating aboveground, and as a result the structure interrupts the topography very little.

The glass-enclosed front facade makes the house appear transparent and lets the occupants see far into the distant surroundings.

The simplicity that characterizes the exterior and its beautiful woodwork flows into the interior. Stairs are placed along a longitudinal wall across from a galley kitchen, freeing the view to the living and seating area. The second level houses the bedrooms, arranged in a mezzanine, from which one can have a panoramic view. In an effort to reveal the nature of the building's construction materials, interior and exterior details were designed to expose as much of every framing member as possible. In so doing, even the exterior wallboard reveals its true panelized nature. According to Cutler Anderson Architects, their intention was "to honor each material, including flashing, so they could tell their story and add a richness of comprehensible detail to the owners' experience."

Front view

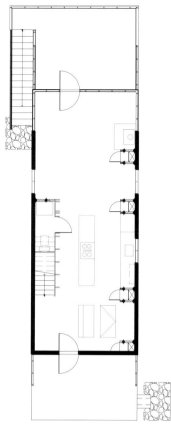

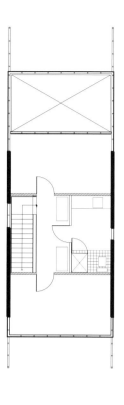

Ground floor ⌐————⌐ 7'

Second floor

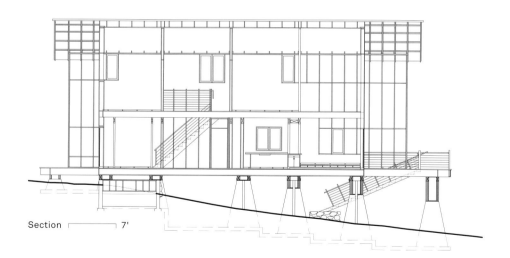

Section ⌐————⌐ 7'

top: Perspective view
bottom: Side view

Night view

top: View from second floor
bottom: Kitchen and living areas

# GLASS SHUTTER HOUSE

**Width: 13 ft.**

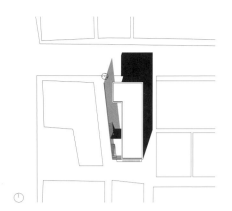

LOCATION
**Setagaya**
**Tokyo, Japan**

DESIGNER
**Shigeru Ban Architects**

COMPLETION
**2005**

FOOTPRINT
**676 sq. ft. (63.6 sq. m)**

FLOOR AREA
**793 sq. ft. (73.7 sq. m)**

The Glass Shutter House was commissioned by a television chef who needed a restaurant and studio for taping his program and a residence for himself, his wife, and his daughter. The 13-by-52-foot (4-by-16-meter) structure accomodates these functions imaginatively.

Because the front half of the site faces a public road, the architect adhered to a regulation mandating a two-story height limit. The perimeter walls are clad in aluminum-framed glass shutters that can be rolled up and stored in metal containers on the roof.

The openness lends a lightness to the entire building. Explaining the internal arrangement of restaurant, living spaces, and studio-kitchen, Ban explains, "The three elements put into a diagram would be like the overlapping rings of the Mastercard symbol."

The transparency between indoor and outdoor areas is further enhanced by the use of two- and three-story curtains. Ban says, "It becomes possible to create situations to adapt to varying seasons and occasions, just as we change clothing accordingly."

The interior is minimalist in style. Whereas the ground floor has a restaurant layout, the second floor houses another kitchen and dining area, as well as a rear bedroom. On the third floor is the master bedroom suite and an eating and sleeping space lined with tatami mats.

above: Site plan
opposite: Ground-floor restaurant

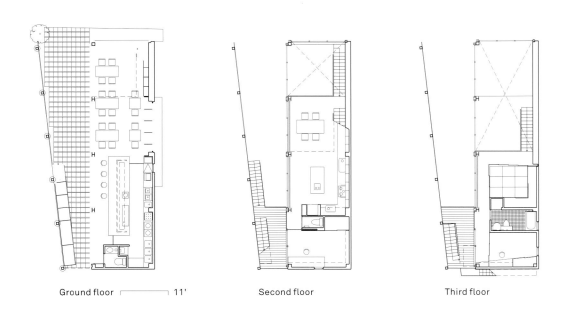

Ground floor ⌐———⌐ 11'          Second floor          Third floor

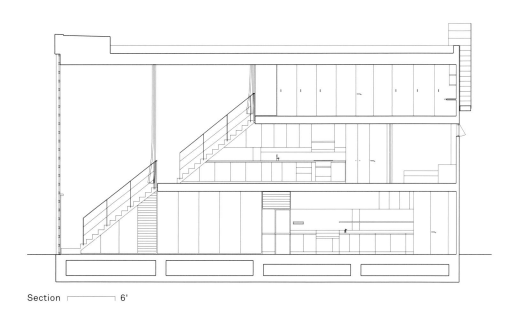

Section ⌐———⌐ 6'

Street view

Courtyard

View through the floors

# HERAN HOUSE

Width: 14 ft.

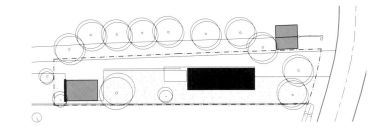

LOCATION
**Ghent, Belgium**

DESIGNER
**Caan Architecten**

COMPLETION
**2005**

FOOTPRINT
**952 sq. ft. (89 sq. m)**

FLOOR AREA
**1,180 sq. ft. (109 sq. m)**

The design challenge for the Heran House was to conceive of a dwelling for a 20-foot-wide (6-meter) lot, with a passage remaining to reach another house behind it.

Due to privacy concerns, the daytime functions (kitchen and living room) were placed on the first floor. By introducing a band of windows around the house, the occupants were given a panoramic view of the neighboring front gardens.

The heights of different floors influenced the arrangement of interior spaces. A family room, TV-viewing area, and library was placed halfway underground on the lower level, offering additional privacy.

The designers located the service functions, which include plumbing and storage areas, in a central core, thereby leaving free space around it.

Three bedrooms are clustered at the rear of the second floor. A small patio separates them from the bathroom and dressing room. Interestingly, this patio is used as an exterior shower hidden from the lower level.

The clean exterior, clad with brick and untreated wood, includes an expansive window. The home fits the context nicely and has a sculptural quality.

above: Site plan
opposite: Front view

1 Entrance
2 Vestibule
3 Storage
4 Closet
5 Laundry
6 Counter
7 Fireplace
8 TV-viewing area
9 Library
10 Living room
11 Dining room
12 Kitchen
13 Storage
14 Powder room
15 Hallway and dressing area
16 Bathroom
17 Shower
18 Patio
19 Master bedroom
20 Children's bedroom

Lower floor |———| 10'

First floor

Second floor

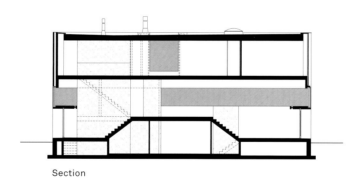

Section

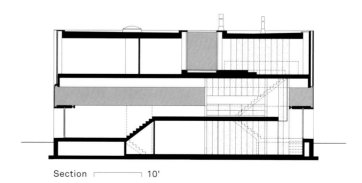

Section |———| 10'

top: View of the front yard
bottom left: Night view from street

bottom middle: Rear view
bottom right: Facade detail

Hallway

Bathroom

Dining and living areas

# MODERN
# WOODEN TOWN

Width: 20 ft.

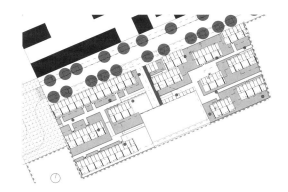

LOCATION
**Porvoo, Finland**

DESIGNER
**Tuomo Siitonen Architects**

COMPLETION
**2005**

SITE AREA
**11.1 acres (4.5 hectares)**

FOOTPRINT
**720 sq. ft. (66 sq. m)**

FLOOR AREA
**430.6 sq. ft. (40 sq. m)**

A walk along the Porvoo River in the city of Porvoo, Finland, offers a striking resemblance between the historic and the recently added modern dwellings. This project is a splendid example of weaving old and new. Color choice—red ochre boiled paint—is also a reminder that innovation and tradition are not contradictory terms.

The approach to the site, which is bounded by a river on one side and a park on the other, encompasses principles of walkability and green features such as recycling and composting bins. The lack of car dominance becomes apparent with the prominence of weblike pedestrian paths that connect a variety

of dwelling types. A parking structure is suitably located in the middle of the cluster, a short distance away from each home.

The two-story-tall dwelling featured here defines public and private outdoor areas. Attention was paid to the placement of openings to enhance passive solar gain. These dwellings are constructed on grade, with shallow foundations providing direct access to the yard.

Architect Tuomo Siitonen crafted the design of the narrow interior by creating atriumlike, two-story open spaces that expand the volume vertically. The stairs are in proximity to the entrance for better interior circulation. Two optional layouts were designed, with living areas, utility functions, and one bedroom on the ground floor. Additional bedrooms and bathrooms are located on the second floor. Both options use an open-plan concept, which further makes relatively small spaces seem larger.

above: Site plan

top: View from the street
bottom: A row of dwellings

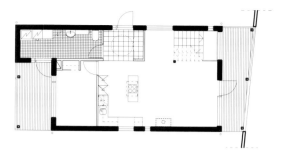

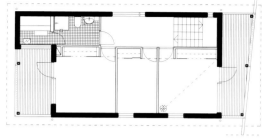

Option 1: Ground floor ⌐———⌐ 8'

Second floor

View from the Porvoo River

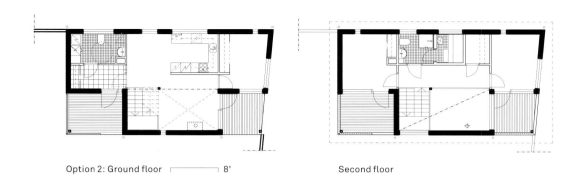

Option 2: Ground floor    ⊢──────⊣  8'          Second floor

top: View from the Porvoo River
bottom: Street view

Exterior facade details

# LANEWAY HOUSE

**Width: 18 ft.**

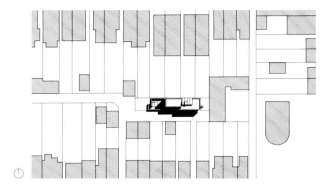

LOCATION
**Toronto
Ontario, Canada**

DESIGNER
**Shim-Sutcliffe Architects**

COMPLETION
**1993**

FOOTPRINT
**864 sq. ft. (80.3 sq. m)**

FLOOR AREA
**1,350 sq. ft. (125 sq. m)**

In addition to being beautifully designed, Laneway House offers an intriguing and much-needed urban solution. Within the city of Toronto, an extensive network of laneways service the rear portions of residential neighborhoods. A derelict site within this intense urban condition was the starting point for a single-family residence.

In stark contrast to its context and surrounded by a concrete garden wall that wraps around the property and protects a wooden pavilion within it, the house is conceived as a series of interior and exterior gardens and courts. Rich textural materials and pivoting window planes blur the relationship between inside and out.

The building was designed for a typical Toronto lot and Victorian house typology, with its limitations of narrow width and poor lighting conditions. This dwelling addresses and transforms these common constraints in a delightful way.

The designers managed to alleviate the feeling of a small space. A water feature in the rear court flows nicely into the interior. The back-facing dining room takes advantage of this opening and that of a skylight to bring daylight into the home's core and increase the sense of spaciousness. The simple minimalist design and mix of materials make the dwelling unique from an urban and architectural point of view.

above: Site plan
opposite: Entrance at night

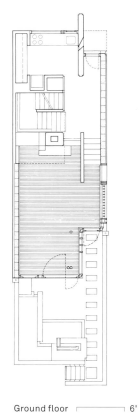
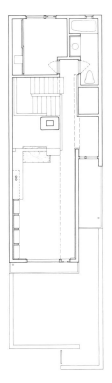

Ground floor ⌐———⌐ 6'     Second floor

bottom left: Side view
bottom right: Skylight

top left: Fireplace
top right: Water feature in winter

bottom: Dining room

# WEBSTER RESIDENCE

Width: 25 ft.

LOCATION

**Venice Beach
California, United States**

DESIGNER

**Ehrlich Architects**

COMPLETION

**2003**

SITE AREA

**0.08 acre (0.03 hectare)**

FOOTPRINT

**2,625 sq. ft. (243.2 sq. m)**

FLOOR AREA

**1,800 sq. ft. (167.2 sq. m)**

Located in the heart of Venice Beach, California, this residence features an inner courtyard in the middle of a narrow lot, with buildings on either end linked by a passageway. The designers therefore suggested an inward-looking scheme in which the living areas define a central core. Introducing terraces on the second floor, in the front and back of the main building, offers airiness to the rooms. The rear portion of the house is slightly elevated, while the lower level includes a garage with an entrance from an alleyway.

The glass-front living area, which is somewhat lower than street level, and the open-space concept in the kitchen create a flow of space into the rear court. The use of metal link walkways contributes to the lightness of the court. Glass roll-up doors facing the court-yard and the front entrance allow for an uninterrupted view through the ground floor. Polished concrete floors, light-colored fireplace covers, and white bookshelves add to the sense of spaciousness.

above: Site plan

Rear elevation

Lower level ⌐————⌐ 21'    Ground floor          Second floor          Roof plan

bottom left: View of the rear living area
bottom right: Outdoor court

Living area

# HARLESS RESIDENCE

**Width: 24 ft.**

LOCATION

**Manhattan Beach
California, United States**

DESIGNER

**Dean Nota Architect**

COMPLETION

**2004**

SITE AREA

**0.036 acre (0.01 hectare)**

FLOOR AREA

**2,241 sq. ft. (208 sq. m)**

Located in a beachfront community on the western edge of metropolitan Los Angeles, this house offers views of adjacent rooftops and the Pacific Ocean. The narrow 30-by-52-foot (9-by-16-meter) lot is situated three blocks from the beach in a dense neighborhood of eclectic homes. It is served by a local street to the north and an alley to the south.

The three-level house has a main entry, family room, and parking on the ground floor; three private bedrooms on the first floor; and living, dining, and kitchen on the second floor. Spaces open up horizontally to the front and rear from a central service core.

The house's form reflects a collection of neighborhood elements, with attention to light, view, and climate. Street elevations are symmetrically organized and composed of stucco, glass, and concrete blocks. A steel-framed cantilevered deck evokes the image of local fishing piers. This combination of familiar elements is topped by folded metal planes and a glazed window wall.

The spatial experience unfolds in sequence, as one moves from a modest entry through the building. Moving up the stairs reveals a succession of spaces that become progressively more dynamic, with increasing light and views. Living, dining, and kitchen areas are located below the folded roof, and wall planes leaning to the north and south visually extend these spaces beyond the site's perimeter.

Sustainable strategies were an integral part of the design. The dwelling uses a combination of high-performance glazing and insulation, efficient mechanical and electrical systems, and internal sun-control shades with passive energy techniques to make it compatible with California's energy code. Passive techniques include exposed concrete floors and masonry walls to store thermal energy, thereby reducing heating requirements and eliminating the need for air conditioning. All structural framing members and sheathing were manufactured from engineered, sustainable-growth and reclaimed wood. Cedar beams in the roof trellis, harvested from certified domestic sources, are the only sawn lumber.

Front view

Third floor

Second floor

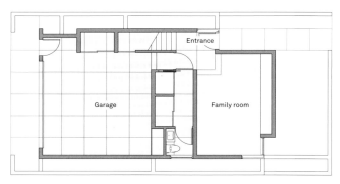

Ground floor ⊢────── 9'

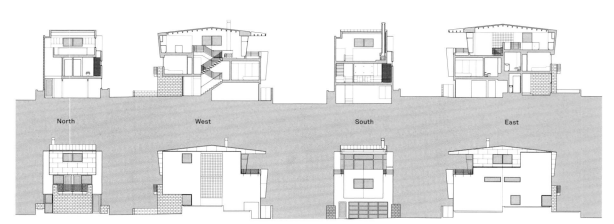

Sections and elevations

top: Rear view
bottom: Living room

top: Family room
bottom: Master bathroom

View of stairs

top: Living room
bottom: Dining and living areas

Front view at night

# GALLEY HOUSE

**Width: 12 ft.**

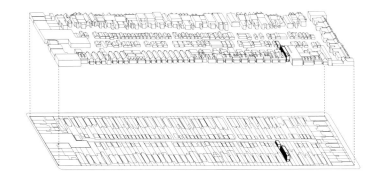

LOCATION
**Toronto**
**Ontario, Canada**

DESIGNER
**Donald Chong Studio**

COMPLETION
**2006**

SITE AREA
**2,180 sq. ft. (202 sq. m)**

FOOTPRINT
**744 sq. ft. (70.3 sq. m)**

FLOOR AREA
**815 sq. ft. (75 sq. m)**

The Galley House is an infill project situated on a long, narrow lot. The design challenge was to conceive a detached dwelling offering comfortable space, ample natural light, and interior and exterior views.

This three-story, single-family unit measures 12 by 62 feet (3.7 by 19 meters). Due to municipal code constraints, there are no windows on the side walls. According to the designer, one aim of the project was "to take advantage of the existing city infrastructure, thereby reducing urban sprawl."

The interior includes living functions on the ground floor and a double-height family room that opens to the street. Three bedrooms are located on the second floor, while the third floor houses the master bedroom suite. The clean lines that characterize the interior add an air of simplicity that is typical of the entire design. Glass guardrails make the space feel uncluttered and wide. A beautifully landscaped rear court contributes to the sense of an urban oasis.

above: Site overview
opposite: Exterior view from the south

Garage

Garden court

Kitchen (below)

Dining room

Living room

Ground floor 8'

Bedroom

Bedroom

Family room

Second floor

Roof deck

Master bedroom

Open to below

Third floor

top: Front porch and entrance
bottom: Rear court

Kitchen

Interior view

# SUISSE OPTION HOME

Width: 13 ft.

LOCATION
**Switzerland**

DESIGNER
**Bauart Architekten und
Planer**

COMPLETION
**2001**

FOOTPRINT
**430.7 sq. ft. (40.2 sq. m)**

FLOOR AREA
**178 sq. ft. (63 sq. m)**

Somewhat different than the other projects, the Suisse Option Home is prefabricated and can be located anywhere. The dimensions of the structure are based on highway transportation requirements in addition to functionality.

The design is the outcome of a collaboration between designers and fabricators attempting to achieve a high quality-per-cost ratio. The home is composed of two equal-sized boxes that are transported to a building site and placed on a 13-by-33-foot (4-by-10-meter) prelaid foundation in less than a day.

Interior space was optimized by placing the wet functions and stairs in the module's center. The area devoted to circulation was also minimized as a result. Four large exterior windows make the small space feel bigger and extend the indoors outward.

The designers envisioned a dwelling unit that would accommodate various functions and users, such as serving as an extension to an existing house, as a space for a small household, or as a home office. The chosen colors help define the interior and offer uniqueness to each space.

Perspective view

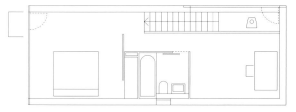

Second floor

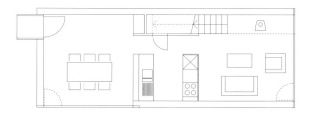

Ground floor ⌐‾‾‾‾‾⌐ 6'

middle left: Off-site fabrication

middle right: On-site installation
bottom right: View of kitchen space

top: Longitudinal sections
bottom: Interior view

Exterior view

top: Rear view
bottom: Side view

# VH R-10 gHOUSE

Width: 16 ft.

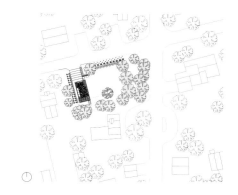

LOCATION

**Vineyard Haven
Massachusetts, United States**

DESIGNER

**Darren Petrucci**

COMPLETION

**2007**

FOOTPRINT

**640 sq. ft. (58.8 sq. m)**

FLOOR AREA

**1,400 sq. ft. (130 sq. m)**

The need to design a dwelling that can be fabricated in one place and erected in another was the guiding principle behind the VH R-10 gHouse, as well as the desire to maximize the area permitted for guesthouses according to local zoning. In effect, it's an infill project that fits nicely into the local context. According to the architect, the 600-square-foot (56-square-meter) first floor was established as 5.5 feet (1.7 meters) above ground, thereby raising the basement a half level and creating easy walking and car access to the garage. Even though the living area is raised, the 24-foot (7.3-meter) height restriction accommodated a double-space interior.

Access to the basement was created by dividing the dwelling into three volumes. The middle volume, for living and dining, shifts 4 feet (1.2 meters) outward to make room for vertical circulation. The exteriors are wrapped in a wooden rainscreen, thereby creating a layered extension of the interior while providing weather protection and privacy barriers.

Construction of the dwelling included premanufactured building techniques that were modified to meet local codes. Oriented strand board was used for the floor and roof deck. The main structure is built with SIPs on a 4-foot (1.2-meter) module. The entire structure was assembled in three days, including a 40-foot (12-meter) engineered beam for the sliding screen cantilevers.

above: Site plan

Perspective view

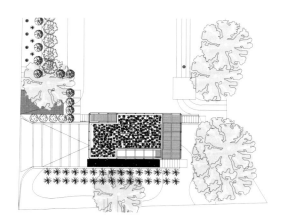

Roof plan

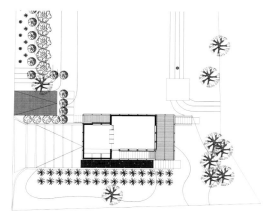

Second floor

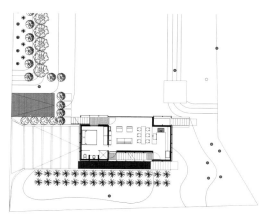

First floor

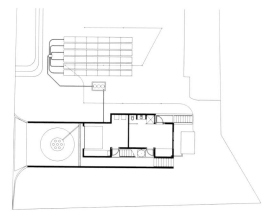

Lower level ⌐————⌐ 21'

top: View of roof garden
bottom: Living area

top: Exterior detail
bottom: View at dusk

top: Side elevations with shutters open and closed
bottom: Side view at dusk

top: Double-height living area
bottom: Interior views

View from kitchen

# SLIT HOUSE

**Width: 14 ft.**

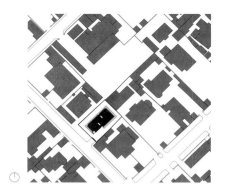

LOCATION
**Nanjing**
**Jiangsu, China**

DESIGNER
**AZL Atelier Zhanglei**

COMPLETION
**2007**

FOOTPRINT
**294 sq. ft. (27.5 sq. m)**

FLOOR AREA
**807 sq. ft. (75 sq. m)**

The sculptural quality of the Slit House is instantly apparent. Built of concrete and timber, the structure is made up of interlocking volumes arranged to let light in through narrow side openings. The front facade has a square window that lights an attic-level library and reading room. The floor below it houses a bedroom. Another bedroom can be found on the ground floor, where daytime functions, including the living, dining, and kitchen spaces, are also located.

For construction efficiency, the architect located the stairs and service core at the center, leaving the edges for either living spaces or bedrooms. According to the architect, this is the first real concrete house in Nanjing, which has seen its skyline transform in recent years with the introduction of some 1,300 high-rise structures.

above: Site plan
opposite: Southeast view

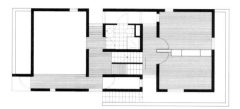

Second floor

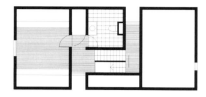

Fourth floor

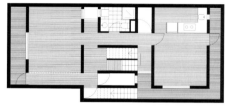

Ground floor ⊢———⊣ 5'

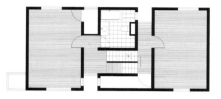

Third floor

bottom: East view

Front elevation

left: Dining space
right: View through side window

Living area

# S.H.

Width: 25 ft.

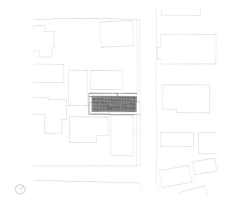

### LOCATION
**Takarazuka**
**Hyogo, Japan**

### DESIGNER
**Katsuhiro Miyamoto &
Associates**

### COMPLETION
**2003**

### SITE AREA
**0.03 acre (0.01 hectare)**

### FOOTPRINT
**1,504.8 sq. ft. (139.8 sq. m)**

### FLOOR AREA
**343.6 sq. ft. (31.9 sq. m)**

The S.H. is an infill project constructed in a hilly 1950s neighborhood. The client, a married couple, are university professors. The house's name, in fact, is derived from the initials of their nicknames. The need to design on a narrow lot and accommodate a nonconventional program led to an interesting layout. In addition to having a kitchen, dining area, and bathroom on the ground floor, a study area with plenty of bookshelves occupies approximately 30 percent of that level. The clients regard that space as their laboratory.

The design offers a variety of interesting interior views by creating unique combinations of volumes between floors. It results in a clever manipulation of the structure's height. The space became even more efficient by using the wall area. Shelves of different sizes and forms cover the walls, which satisfied the daily storage needs of the occupants.

It is clear from examining the design that its uniqueness is an outcome of knowing how to work with volumes rather than plans. Simplicity and elimination of redundancy is another characteristic of this eloquent design.

above: Site plan
opposite: View from carport

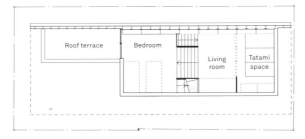

Second floor

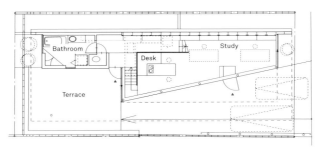

Ground floor ⌐────────┐ 10'

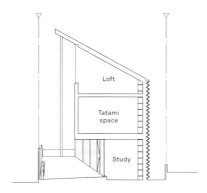

North/south section

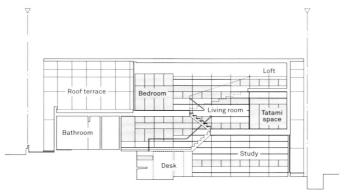

East/west section

View from west

Interior views

Night view of interior

# TOWNHOUSES

The projects featured in this section can be divided into two groups. The first is the conversion of older structures to contemporary uses, and the second is the insertion of new buildings into an existing urban fabric. The objectives of the designers in the second category were to reduce footprints, lower costs, and create a pleasing assembly. As such, attention was paid to privacy, outdoor spaces, avoiding monotony, letting light into the core of the middle units, and making efficient use of a relatively small space. Several design strategies were used to attain these goals, including the use of color as well as glass on the facades as a means to open a dark interior to the outdoors. When the conversion of an old structure to new uses was undertaken, working with the existing facade was mandated, and the functions that abutted it had to be designed accordingly. Not having side windows was another distinguishing aspect of these projects. Light could only be brought in from the front and the rear. In architecture, constraints are often reasons for innovation, which is reflected in the designs assembled here. The use of glass partitions on the interior to avoid the need for solid walls, as well as the intro- duction of skylights, were some of the means these designers used.

# KANAMORI HOUSE

**Width: 9 ft.**

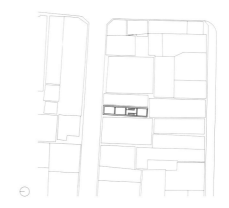

LOCATION
**Osaka, Japan**

DESIGNER
**Tadao Ando Architects & Associates**

COMPLETION
**1994**

SITE AREA
**621.9 sq. ft. (57.8 sq. m)**

FOOTPRINT
**465.5 sq. ft. (43.5 sq. m)**

FLOOR AREA
**468.2 sq. ft. (43.5 sq. m)**

Fitting a dwelling and a business into a 9.5-foot-wide (2.9-meter) and 49-foot-long (15-meter) lot was the urban challenge faced by architect Tadao Ando. A four-story structure that accommodates an arts-and-crafts store on the ground level and a residence on the upper floors was the outcome. The exterior concrete forms are held in place with special pads, which were not removed because the exterior walls were constructed very close to the lot line. The urban site also posed a logistical challenge and required the cooperation of neighbors during construction.

Letting in natural light was another challenge. The architect, renowned for his signature exposed-concrete buildings, such as the TOTO Seminar House, chose to address this challenge by creating a rectangle divided into four parts, with two- and three-story vertical voids. The voids expose each room to light as well as serve as spatial extensions of each room's area. The use of the narrow space was made efficient by placing the stairs along the longitudinal walls, which, according to the architect, "gave the residential quarters a mazelike quality." Light enters the building through the vertically extended street facade, clad with frosted glass, which offers indoor privacy. The front elevation is divided into four equal rectangular segments, lending simplicity and elegance to the structure's facade. This design strategy contrasts a lighter street front with a heavier interior.

above: Site plan
opposite: Street elevation

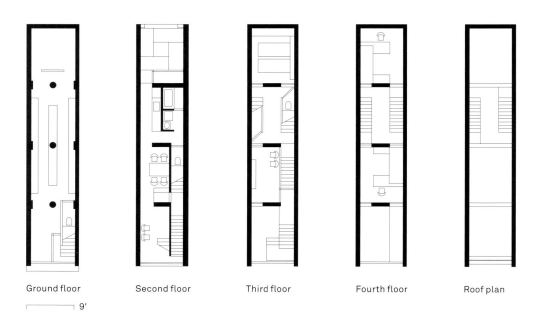

Ground floor      Second floor      Third floor      Fourth floor      Roof plan

⌐———┐ 9'

Views of ground floor

Views of courtyard

# TOWNHOUSE IN DC

Width: 18 ft.

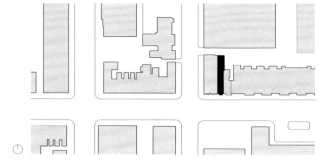

LOCATION
**Washington DC**
**United States**

DESIGNER
**Robert M. Gurney**

COMPLETION
**2007**

SITE AREA
**0.04 acres (0.02 hectares)**

FOOTPRINT
**1,800 sq. ft. (165 sq. m)**

FLOOR AREA
**1,800 sq.ft. (167.2 sq.m)**

This townhouse is located in a historic district in Washington DC and forms part of a row of structures. The 18-foot-wide (5.5-meter), 100-foot-long (30-meter) building backs onto a lane in a gridiron urban pattern. The building was previously used as commercial space on all three floors and occupied the entire lot. The height of each level is 9 feet (2.7 meters) and was subject to previous rounds of renovations.

As required by local bylaws, the architect kept the original limestone facade, which is well-proportioned and retains its elegant stonework and details. The ground floor was left for commercial use, with a separate entrance to a store resembling a traditional townhouse.

Another challenge the architect faced was to bring light and a sense of airiness to the building's core. This was largely achieved by adding a skylight and removing sections of the floor, which also contributed to the flow of space between levels. A section of the third floor was removed to accommodate a stair. Above the steel-and-aluminum stair, a rooftop addition opens to adjacent terraces and provides outdoor spaces and views. During renovation, a majority of the original floor joists were retained in an effort to reuse the existing structure and to avoid disturbing the limestone facade.

The architect used an open plan to craft the interior and to further enhance the daylighting of rooms. Interior partitions are made of clear glass. The minimalist design of these partitions helps make the interior spaces seem less cluttered. Exposed brick walls, which are painted white, are a suitable contrast to the blue epoxy floors. Glass and steel elements in the interior result in a modern spatial quality within this traditional structure.

above: Site plan
opposite: Street view

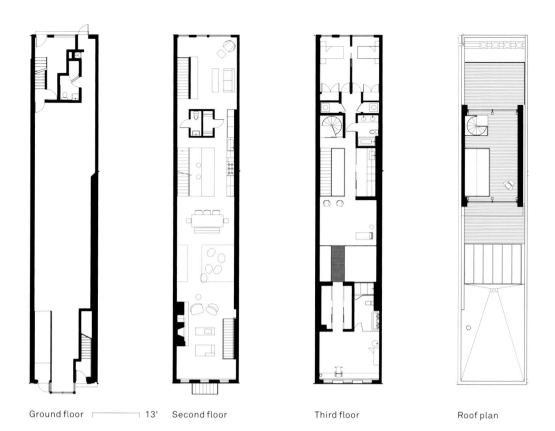

Ground floor ┌─────┐ 13'    Second floor         Third floor          Roof plan

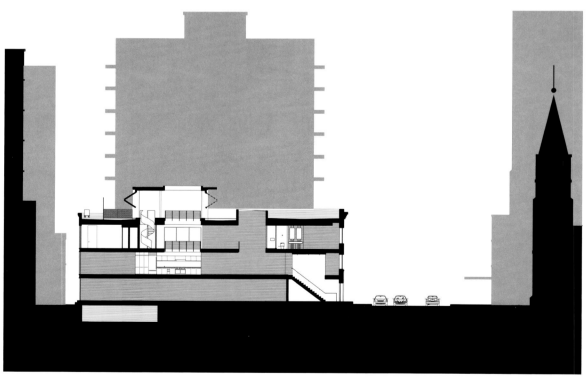

Site section

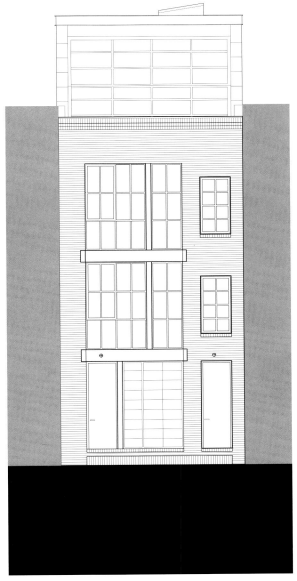

Street elevation ⌐——⌐ 5'

Alley elevation

top right: Bedroom suite

bottom left: View from the kitchen
bottom right: Dining and living areas

View through central core

# FITCH/O'ROURKE RESIDENCE

Width: 17 ft.

LOCATION
**Washington DC
United States**

DESIGNER
**Robert M. Gurney**

COMPLETION
**2001**

SITE AREA
**0.04 acres (0.02 hectares)**

FOOTPRINT
**1,071 sq. ft. (988 sq. m)**

FLOOR AREA
**1,660 sq. ft. (154.2 sq. m)**

This townhouse, located in the Adams Morgan/Kalorama Heights section of Washington DC, was for many years a neighborhood eyesore. The renovation transformed it into a thoroughly modern, warm, and intimate residence with light-filled two- and three-story open spaces and a mix of innovative materials.

The previous owner had gutted the interior and demolished the entire back wall of the townhouse before a zoning dispute stopped his effort to convert it into a multiunit condominium. For the next several years, before being purchased by the current clients, the building remained empty, filled with debris and exposed to the elements. Unfortunately, nothing indoors was worth saving.

The new owners viewed the property as a rare opportunity to build a completely modern residence in an established neighborhood. Their program included a two-bedroom, two-study residence (convertible into three bedrooms and a study) on the upper three levels, and a one-bedroom rental unit in the basement. The clients wanted a home that would fit the urban context but remain intimate.

The project faced three constraints: the house's long, narrow footprint, measuring 63 by 17 feet (19 by 5.2 meters), which was narrowed down to 13 feet (4 meters) in width, dictated an in-line room arrangement; the property's location in a designated historic district required the front facade be kept intact; and the client's limited budget, which lowered the project's cost to about $140 per square foot ($1,500 per square meter).

The renovation, beginning with two brick sidewalls and a dirt-floor basement, amounted to constructing a new house inside an old shell. The design altered the building's narrow confines by combining a traditional orthogonal scheme with curving geometry, where most curves and radials trace back to a center point located 28 feet (8.5 meters) east of the house and a rotation space based on a 10-degree diagonal line running from a rear corner to the center of the dining room.

The living room takes advantage of the southern exposure and the opportunity to build a new rear facade to bring light into its loftlike space, while another space near the front brings light into the northern end. Materials were carefully chosen to create a rich, warm mixture of colors and textures that also modulate the incoming light. These include concrete, steel, block aluminum, lead-coated copper, copper wire cloth, UNA-CLAD corrugated panels, clear and sandblasted glass, Kalwall and Lumicite translucent panels, limestone tile, Kirkstone and limestone countertops, maple and mahogany veneer cabinets and wall panels, and maple and Brazilian cherry flooring.

opposite: Renovated rear elevation

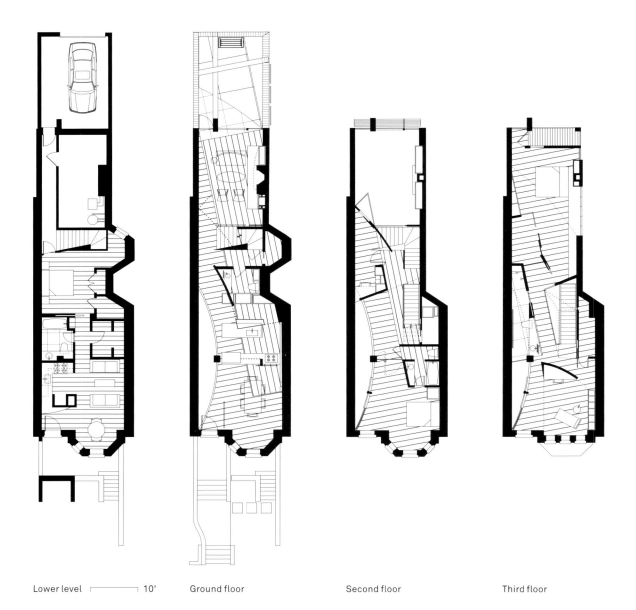

Lower level ┌──────┐ 10'    Ground floor                    Second floor                    Third floor

top left: View of living room
top right: View toward stair

bottom left: Downward view of front door
bottom right: View of courtyard

Interior view

top: Bedroom

bottom left: Kitchen
bottom right: Dining room

# T RESIDENCE

Width: 21 ft.

LOCATION
**New York**
**New York, United States**

DESIGNER
**Studio Rinaldi**

COMPLETION
**2003**

SITE AREA
**2,500 sq. ft. (232 sq. m)**

FLOOR AREA
**2,500 sq. ft. (232 sq. m)**

Letting in daylight and marrying old and new are the trusts of the T Residence design. Located in Manhattan's Upper West Side in New York, this renovation preserves the townhouse's old features, such as its plaster ceiling and crown molding in the dining room, and it integrates newer materials like Plexiglas in the garden.

The architect has chosen to locate the day functions on the ground floor of the two-story flat, which is part of a five-story structure. The dining room, configured in an open plan concept, is set near the kitchen and fits nicely with the bay created by the facade. A rear stairway connects the first and second levels, which contain the bedrooms. The rear elevation features a balcony overlooking the courtyard. By glazing the dwelling's rear facade, a spatial flow to the outside was achieved, an aspect that makes the interior seem larger. Transparency was gained indoors by using glass partitions and doors that, although they serve to separate the functions and spaces, do not block the passage of light. Sandblasted polycarbonate stair risers and shelves, as well as clear polycarbonate vertical elements in the study, project light from the exterior.

Oak, which was used in the original design, was selected for the dining room, vestibule, study, bedrooms, and den, achieving integration of old and new. The wood floors and baseboards are clear white oak, and the flooring differentiates the traditional central living room, where much of the original detailing is preserved. A walnut border and diagonal plank installation subtly set off the living room, while the new doors adjacent to the existing fireplace blend into the wall with painted stucco work and oak panels.

The garden can be regarded as the last room of the townhouse. The small space embraces many different materials and textures. On the walls, rough and natural Brazilian quartzite contrasts with polished French limestone. Elements of the garden include a teak bench, steel channels, various pavers, and a concrete fountain.

opposite: Rear elevation

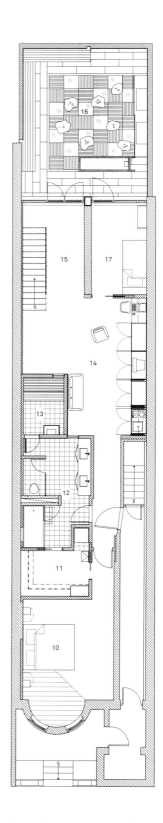

Ground floor &#9500;&#9472;&#9472;&#9472;&#9472;&#9488; 7'

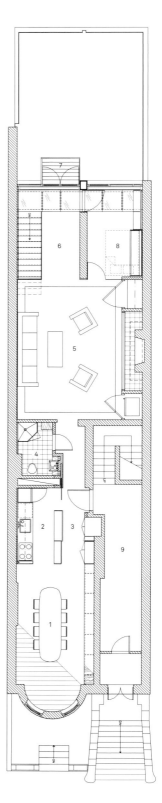

Second floor

left and opposite:
1   Dining room
2   Kitchen
3   Entry hall
4   Powder room
5   Living room
6   Landing
7   Balcony
8   Study
9   Public corridor
10   Master bedroom
11   Master closet
12   Master bathroom
13   Sauna
14   Den
15   Landing
16   Courtyard
17   Guest bedroom

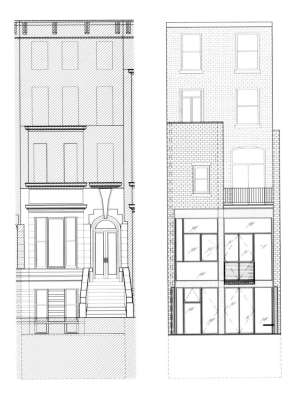

Front elevation                    Rear elevation

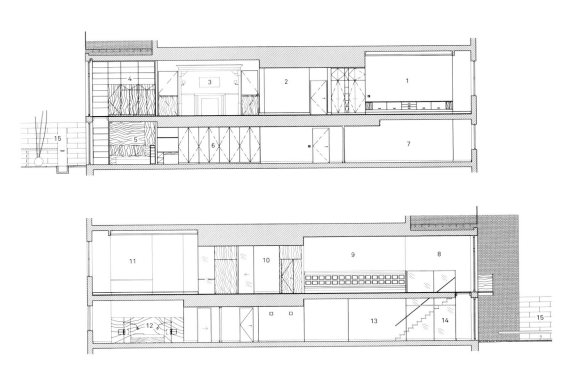

Sections ⌐──── 15'

Views of courtyard

Interior views

top: Study alcove in the closed and open positions
bottom: Living room

Interior detail of the study

# WOHNPARK AM BETZENBERG

Width: 20 ft.

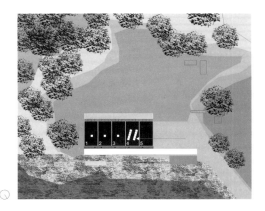

LOCATION
**Kaiserslautern, Germany**

DESIGNER
**AV1 Architekten Butz Dujmovic Schanné Urig**

COMPLETION
**2000**

SITE AREA
**1.7 acres (0.7 hectare)**

FOOTPRINT
**5 dwelling units:**
**3,230 sq. ft. (300 sq. m)**

FLOOR AREA
**1 dwelling unit:**
**645.8 sq. ft. (60 sq. m)**

A unique feature of this project is its chosen location and the relation of the row to the site. The townhouses are built parallel to a natural wall of red rock. The rock-facing facade is suitably clad with horizontal larch-wood panels, which also cover the north, east, and west elevations, replicating the natural layers visible in the stone. The south elevation is glazed, which both opens the interior to the site's front area and also lets in daylight. The building's roof is equipped with a system that stores rainwater

in one of the layers. The water is heated by solar collectors and the excess is released to the ground to prevent overloading the municipal systems.

The uniqueness of the interior lies in its simplicity. A minimalist approach to the arrangement of space sees the introduction of a single-run staircase that runs crosswise. The stair divides the floors into two zones, with a typical layout on each level: public space in front and private at the rear. The ground floor acts as a mezzanine, open to the space below, and is used as a play or work area. The interior layout, with its open space, gives flexibility to the occupants. A narrow balcony extends the indoors outward and helps cast shadows on the glazed facade, which due to sun angles contributes to passive solar gain in wintertime and reduces cooling requirements in the summer.

above: Site plan

Rear elevations

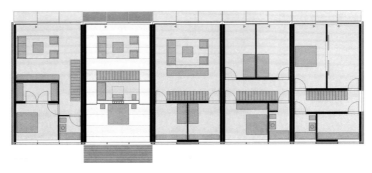

Third floor

Second floor

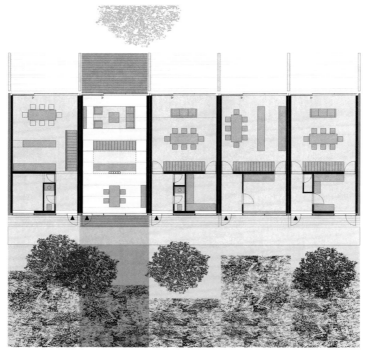

Ground floor ⊢────⊣ 14'

top: Interior view of a typical dwelling unit
bottom: View of entrance and kitchen areas

# BORNEO SPORENBURG

Width: 18 ft.

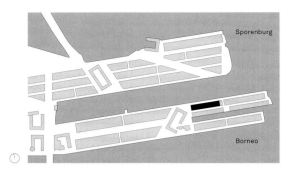

LOCATION
**Amsterdam, the Netherlands**

DESIGNER
**KCAP Architects & Planners**

COMPLETION
**1998**

SITE AREA
**0.7 acre (0.3 hectare)**

FOOTPRINT
**44 dwelling units:**
**66,300 sq. ft. (6,160 sq. m)**

FLOOR AREA
**1 dwelling unit:**
**1,507 sq. ft. (140 sq. m)**

The Borneo Sporenburg area lies in one of Amsterdam's former harbors. The city and the West 8 district planned an urban development with a density of 40 dwellings per acre (100 dwellings per hectare). The area was, therefore, subdivided into strips, and the block on which this project was constructed is part of several elongated tracts of land.

The block is 79 feet (24 meters) deep and unites the two extreme edges of the site. One side looks out across the water, while the other is part of an intimate, urban texture of narrow streets. The back-to-back dwellings have patios and roof terraces, which are used as private outdoor spaces. A parking solution that makes use of internal streets enabled use of the ground-floor level for residential functions, which resulted in lively neighbor relations. The back-to-back dwellings are built above an internal street, which resolves parking issues without having to sacrifice the ground-floor area. Dwellings on the north side are oriented toward the water. With two-story glazed lower facades, they take advantage of the natural light and view. The south-facing dwellings are oriented toward the inner street. Their elevations have a more closed design to ensure privacy. They also have a roof terrace facing an alleyway, which accounts for the staggered frontage.

All the units have a street-facing main door, spacious rooms, and studios on ground level to encourage an engaging outdoor atmosphere. In the living room, a vertical opening facilitates the entry of daylight. The bedroom is situated next to the roof terrace.

This project is an innovative interpretation of the back-to-back townhouse concept that one can find in old European cities, most notably among English terraced housing.

top: Street view
bottom: Rear view

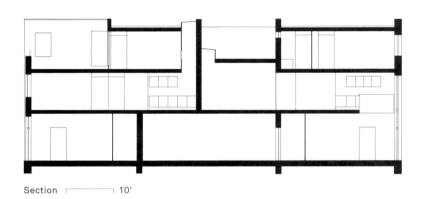

Section ⌐⎯⎯⎯⎯⌐ 10'

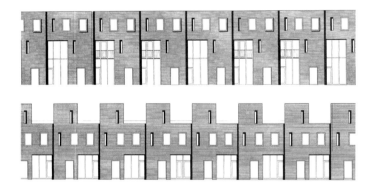

top: Site overview

bottom left: Rear and side elevations
bottom right: Rear facade

Front facade

# EIGHT TERRACED HOUSES

**Width: 12 ft.**

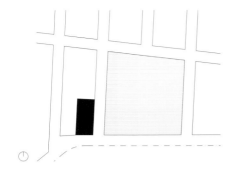

LOCATION
**Totana, Spain**

DESIGNER
**Enrique Mínguez
Martínez Architect**

COMPLETION
**1998**

SITE AREA
**0.1 acre (0.05 hectare)**

FOOTPRINT
**8 dwelling units:
10,968 sq. ft. (1,020 sq. m)**

FLOOR AREA
**1 dwelling unit:
1,371 sq. ft. (127.4 sq. m)**

Eight Terraced Houses was part of the regional government's effort to boost construction and improve the quality of social housing. The designers therefore attempted to break down the poor stigma associated with public housing by choosing an appealing architectural language and relating the row to its urban surroundings.

The designers created an open facade that fits local vernacular and cultural traditions and includes a ground-floor patio and a third-floor terrace. These features also relate the project to the open urban space that it faces and contribute to a lively street life. To further animate the building and street, a range of primary colors—red, blue, and yellow—were chosen.

The openness of the front and rear facades facilitates cross-ventilation, which is much appreciated by the occupants during the hot summer months. Bringing light to the middle of each floor was another challenge faced by the designers. To achieve this, they glazed the second-floor facade, following the minimalist approach taken in the design of the exterior, which nicely continues into each townhouse's interior.

The ground floor houses daytime functions, including the living room and kitchen, for which ample space was provided by placing the stair parallel to the longitudinal wall. The second floor has two bedrooms on opposite ends; another bedroom and a large terrace occupy the third level.

This project demonstrates that social housing need not look glum and that narrow-front dwellings, when well designed, can nicely fit an urban context.

above: Site plan

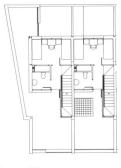

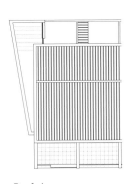

Second floor          Roof plan

Ground floor ⊢————————⊣ 13'          First floor

top: Side elevation
middle left: Street view

bottom left: View of facade

# SLICE HOUSE

**Width: 13 ft.**

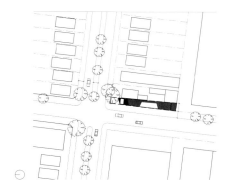

LOCATION
**Porto Alegre, Brazil**

DESIGNER
**Procter-Rihl**

COMPLETION
**2005**

SITE AREA
**1,585 sq. ft. (147.6 sq. m)**

FLOOR AREA
**2,260 sq. ft. (210 sq. m)**

The Slice House was selected to represent Brazil in the 2004 Latin American Architecture Biennale in Lima, Peru. The dwelling is sited on a 12-foot-wide by 126-foot-long (3.7-by-38.5 meter) lot in an established neighborhood. The client, a history professor, asked the architects to design a space for living and entertaining. Originally the program called for a one-bedroom house, which was later changed to two bedrooms, an open living and dining space, a private garden, a master bedroom with ensuite bathroom and generous walk-in closet, and two garage spaces. Natural daylight with solar and ventilation controls were necessary to minimize the need for air conditioning.

Although the building makes reference to modern Brazilian architecture, its form has a contemporary European style with asymmetrical complexity. Vernacular features are expressed in the use of concrete, an open plan, large outdoor spaces, a swimming pool, and a lush garden. The space folds and unfolds within the prismlike form and develops a series of spatial distortions, which create an illusion of greater space on a narrow plot. The walls, tilted seventy degrees, extend the spaces to further achieve an illusion of a larger area.

The upper floor's concrete ceiling folds up or down, defining different spatial zones. The ceiling slopes down in the corridor to a very intimate 6.9-foot (2.1-meter) height near the bedroom door. This creates a forced perspective, which makes the private area of the house appear further away from the social spaces. Turning up the stair and moving into the guestroom and pool lounge, the ceiling continues opening up to the pool terrace and sky. The bedroom is visually enlarged while remaining separate from the front part of the house.

above: Site plan
opposite: Front/side view

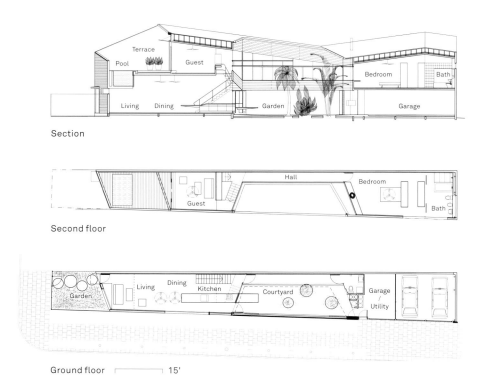

Section

Second floor

Ground floor ⊢————⊣ 15'

View of courtyard

View of entrance

Views of the pool terrace

Living area

# OUTEIRO HOUSE

**Width: 10 ft.**

LOCATION
**Porto, Portugal**

DESIGNER
**Ezzo**

COMPLETION
**2006**

SITE AREA
**603 sq. ft. (56 sq. m)**

FOOTPRINT
**560 sq. ft. (51 sq. m)**

FLOOR AREA
**603 sq. ft. (56 sq. m)**

The earliest records of the construction of the house on Outeiro Street date back to the nineteenth century, at the start of the Romantic era. Built with masonry and wood, the building underwent several modifications and housed different occupants over the years.

At the start of the project, the main facade and the interior wooden beams were the only original elements remaining. The building, 10 feet wide by 56 feet long (3 by 17 meters) on four unevenly sized floors, took up the entire lot. It was decided that all of the existing structural elements would be kept and, from these, a new interior would be built by making use of the floor and assigning a function to each level.

The entrance takes up the entire ground floor, while the bedroom is on the second floor. The third floor is composed of a living room, kitchen, and dining room, leaving the office and terrace for the top floor. The purpose of this distribution was to foster a connection between the house's social areas and the view from the hill on which the dwelling is sited.

To connect spaces, the staircase on the ground floor was hidden in such a way as to not reveal the house's interior. From the second floor to the top, new vertical access points were established using straight-run stairs.

On the ground floor, a coast-sand plaster was used, along with a similar brown-colored material for the exterior so as to create an intimate ambiance. The stairwell, in white, leads into the house, while two pink panels "pop up" along the way, hiding a guest bathroom and a storage room from view.

The second floor has been built using large blocks of yellow granite masonry, which were fitted and then maintained in their entirety, giving this floor a yellowish shade. On the third and fourth floors, built more recently, the walls are smooth and white. The centrally located kitchen creates a unique area that brings the living and dining rooms together, and was designed for socializing and for participating in the ritual of cooking.

opposite: Street view

Third floor

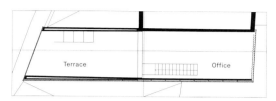

Fourth floor

Ground floor ⊏————⊐ 11'

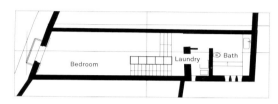

Second floor

Rear facade at night

Interior views
overleaf: View of third floor

# Design Principles

Rooted in past centuries, the narrow house
was a product of necessity, since building in dense
urban areas encouraged land-use efficiency.
Its general layout migrated with the builders who
replicated it throughout the world. Despite its
many countries of origin, the key principles of
narrow house design have remained essentially
unchanged. Generally recognized for its resource
conservation and efficient utilization of space,
the narrow house is attracting home buyers, home
builders, and developers once again. The need to
halt urban sprawl, minimize energy consumption,
and build homes more affordably have refocused
designers' attention on this prototype. This section
defines the significant principles and terms
associated with narrow housing.

## Dwellings for Changing Times

Forms of compact urban housing have been continuously in use throughout human history. From the perspective of recent times, the narrow house is also regarded as an alternative solution to many of our unprecedented environmental problems, some of which are the consequences of urban sprawl.

The proliferation of suburban development is evidence that local human behaviors are having a global impact. In many developed countries, the widespread and extensive use of agricultural and forested land for new housing developments is causing damage to the environment. This condition indicates that humanity is stretching the carrying capacity of the Earth to its limits.

North American domestic water use, for example, almost doubles with outdoor irrigation for larger lot sizes. In many municipalities, overconsumption in residential sectors contributes to two major problems: municipal treatment centers expend large amounts of energy to treat household wastewater, and these centers have no other system with which to manage frequent overloads but to release the excess wastewater untreated into local lakes and rivers. The depletion of freshwater resources is not the only cause for concern; these bodies of water have also become increasingly vulnerable to droughts and floods due to climate change.

The widespread development of detached dwellings, with all sides of a house exposed to the elements, has contributed significantly to the current state of overconsumption. Air conditioners, for example, are estimated to consume as much energy during one summer as all other household appliances combined. The efficient use of building materials, conservation of water, durability and longevity of building components, and better waste management could be implemented through the construction of high-density housing, with less impact on the land.

Due to low-density planning, made possible by cheap fuel, the suburban lifestyle entails a high dependency on cars, but the damage that sprawl is inflicting on the environment is not limited to the effects of automobiles. The popular wood-frame construction of single-family detached homes contributes to deforestation. When two million dwelling units are built every year in the United States, it is worthwhile to reconsider consuming an acre (0.4 hectares) of forest to build a 1,700-square-foot (160-square-meter) home. It has also been demonstrated that an average of 8,000 pounds (3.6 metric tons) of waste are produced when a 2,000-square-foot (190-square-meter) home is constructed, all of which gets shipped to landfills. The worrisome effects of urban sprawl and the overconsumption of natural resources have led to the recognition that fundamental changes to current development patterns are needed, and they should be based on sustainable principles.

The term *sustainable development* began to draw public attention during the late 1960s. Discourse on sustainability revolved around meeting present needs without compromising the ability of future generations to meet theirs. Although these needs were largely undefined, they included social equity, fair distribution of resources within and among nations, and the need to resolve conflicts of interest associated with development pressures and the natural environment. In essence, the objective has been to maintain adequate resources while creating a better world for future generations. This goal can be achieved through a mindset that recognizes the interconnectedness among environmental, economic, social, and cultural concerns.

Especially in architecture, it seems possible to realize this interconnectedness by balancing several factors. There are a number of approaches that support such efforts: the path of least-negative impact, the self-sustaining process, the supporting relationship, and the life cycle approach. The first approach focuses on limiting both the short- and long-term negative impacts of environmental, economic, societal, and cultural factors within a development project. Usually a project's initial impact is given priority. The long-term effects can be viewed as a life cycle. In the simplest of scenarios, this approach can be demonstrated by attaching photovoltaic panels to a house so it serves as an energy generator. Similarly, a house can incorporate a rainwater collection system for producing potable water. As certain systems become independent, others can also work in supporting relationships. Energy generated inside the dwelling, for example, can be used to light communal play areas. This approach requires a heightened sensitivity to patterns of energy use within the home.

In recent years, governments, construction associations, and nongovernmental organizations around the world have begun to set standards for sustainable building practices. These standards go beyond national building codes by establishing stricter criteria for efficiency levels, and in effect they act as accreditation systems. Builders and projects are qualified and distinguished according to the scope of their environmental and sustainable pursuits. In North America, Leadership in Energy and Environmental Design (LEED) was set by the United States Green Building Council (USGBC) and was later adopted by Canada. According to the USGBC, this system is more than a platform for recognition; it is a way of developing sustainable building strategies.

Narrow dwellings, when built in rows, can be considered cohesive sustainable development projects encompassing higher densities. They reduce the need for land allocation to roads, heighten the conservation of energy and other natural resources, allow for mixed land uses, and provide public amenities within walking distance. On the interior, other sustainable aspects naturally fall into place, such as efficient space planning to maximize usable floor area. Simply put, dwellings built closer together result in greater environmental benefits.

## The Family

Parallel to the need to comprehend the interconnectedness of our environmental impacts and the consequences of human actions, there is a need for heightened sensitivity in other areas as well. The family, one of the fundamental building blocks of society, forms the basis of house design. When there are shifts in space usage or in a family's composition or daily habits, these will surely manifest physically in the dwelling itself. In the mid-twentieth century, the post–World War II image of a family composed of the breadwinner father, a stay-at-home mother, and three dependent children was so pervasive that home builders could easily view the bulk of their potential clientele as a homogeneous buying stock. In the eyes of home builders, as well as the average North American citizen, single people rarely bought houses, and families headed by single parents were not serious candidates for homeownership. The majority of people got married in their early twenties and immediately began the search for a house. General expectations of hearth and home were predictable and universally shared. The telecommunications revolution and the widespread use of birth control have added, some might argue, to the continual political weariness, sense of economic impermanence, and apprehension about social values. Developers have noticed shifts in the composition of households, the nature of work and leisure, and the aging population. They have dismissed the concept of the post–World War II homeowner; however, traditional forms of family continue to dominate residential developments. Meanwhile, the population involved in these societal changes has reached a critical mass, validating the alternative approaches explored by policy makers, developers, and architects involved in the conceptualization, design, and marketing of homes.

In response, there has been a rise in the development of housing options that accommodate different types of families and their varying functional and spatial needs within narrower limits or within a single structure; therefore, a diversity of housing stock can exist within a single development. More specifically, the increased number of households and decreased size of the actual family are demographic trends that require housing units for a smaller number of occupants; these units are designed to reflect the changing nature of how occupants group themselves within the home. Moreover, it seems that with fewer people sharing a house, certain assumptions cannot be made about the required house layout. The proportion of divorced couples has steadily climbed, increasing the demand for relocation into lower maintenance, smaller, and more affordable homes, usually within the same municipality. Narrow dwellings, primarily those that can be subdivided to accommodate more than one household, can address these demographic shifts. They should therefore be considered among a range of appropriate solutions.

## Widths and Building Types

A key question when discussing narrow houses is—what is considered narrow? The answer is based on historic precedents, which have been influenced by site conditions, cultural traditions, and technology. On Amsterdam's Singel Street, for example, there is a habitable unit whose front measures 3.3 feet (1 meter). This, of course, is an extremely narrow space, probably a leftover gap between two structures. Analyzing a room's dimensions to ensure its proper functioning is one process for determining the best width of a dwelling. Highway-transit regulations could also be a consideration. When prefabricated, a unit with a width ranging from 14 to 16 feet (4.3 to 4.9 meters) can be shipped from a plant to a construction site without a front- or rear-car escort. A wider structure would be more expensive to deliver.

The minimum width of a dwelling also depends on the creativity of the designer. Past designs show that a 12-foot (3.7-meter) structure built on one to three levels can contain basic amenities. It can accommodate a living room and kitchen on the ground floor, two fair-sized bedrooms on the second, and two more rooms in the basement or attic. The wider the design, the easier it is to fit functions within it. For the sake of this book's definition, dwellings up to 25 feet wide (7.6 meters) qualify as narrow.

Narrow houses can be detached, semidetached (attached on one side), or attached on both sides to form a row. When constructed in rows, they are commonly planned as part of a multistory, multifamily, high-density project. Since their introduction centuries ago, and even more so today, their attraction has remained their groundedness. Whether used by one or several occupants, the design offers easy access to a back or front yard. Unlike apartment living, where a number of occupants share the main door, parking garage, outdoor spaces, and hallways, narrow townhouses offer independence and privacy. The trade-offs include the narrow width, which can restrict interior flexibility, and reduced natural light to middle units. Front and rear yards also tend to be smaller compared to those of detached dwellings.

When cost-effectiveness is sought, choosing a suitable type of dwelling is a high priority. With a cottage, for example, the cost is lowered by building two stories on a single foundation, reducing land and infrastructure expenses. Another option, known as "stuck townhouse," offers further savings by placing two-story dwellings on top of one another. The savings, however, depend on the size of the overall footprint. Choosing a narrow design for these building types would lead to further cost reductions.

An alternative to a narrow single-family building is a multifamily layout with independent dwelling units. This type is known as a duplex when split in two, and a triplex when used by three households. By combining the design attributes of the single-family with "the plex," additional housing types emerge, such as the fourplex, which is essentially two attached duplexes.

Early-twentieth-century
townhouse, Germany

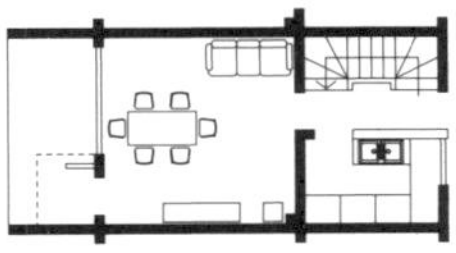

Renaissance townhouse,
United States

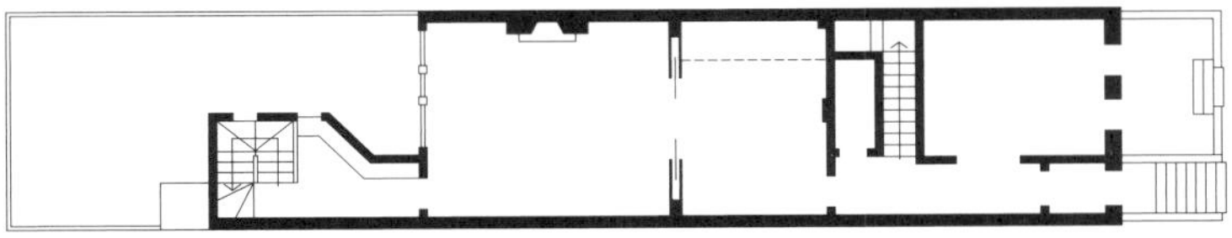

Renaissance townhouse,
England

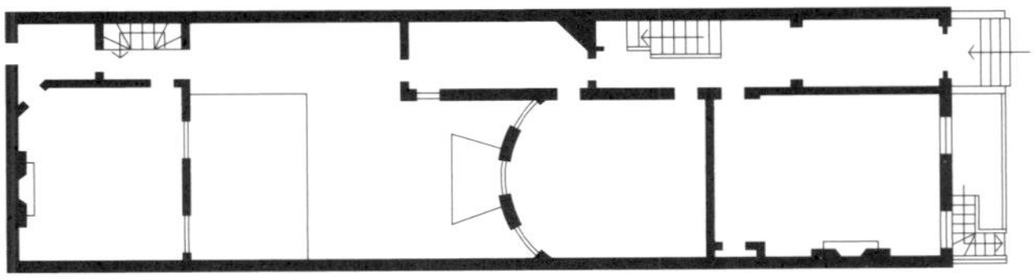

Late-medieval urban house,
England

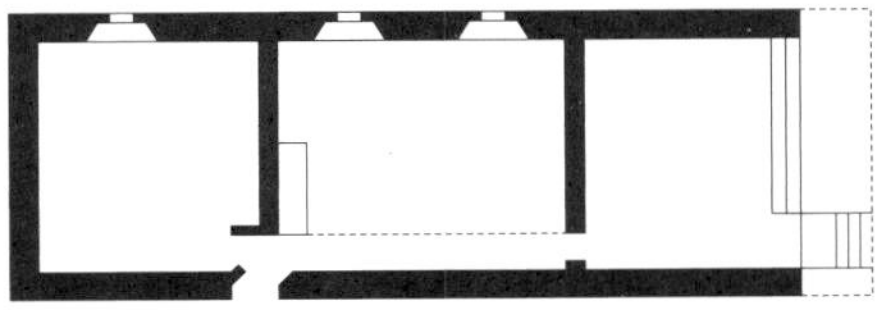

Medieval house, England

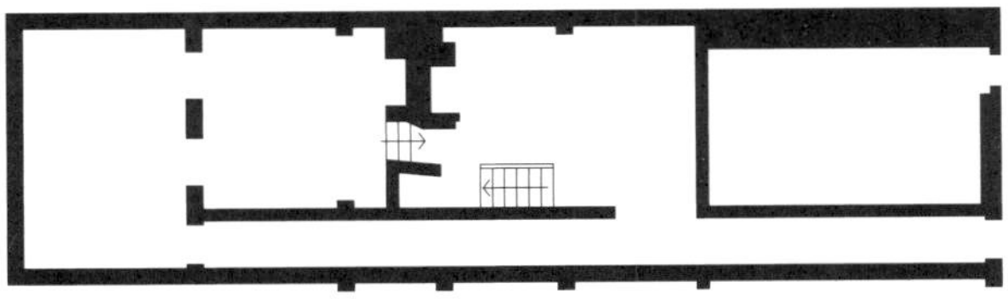

Urban house, India

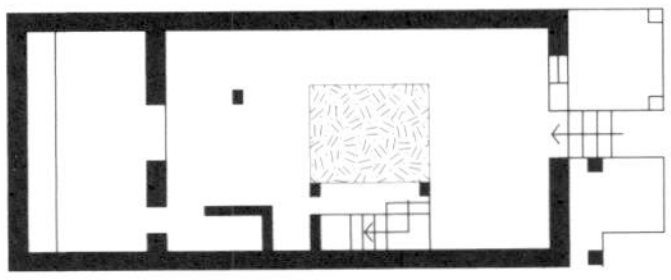

Islamic urban house, Iraq

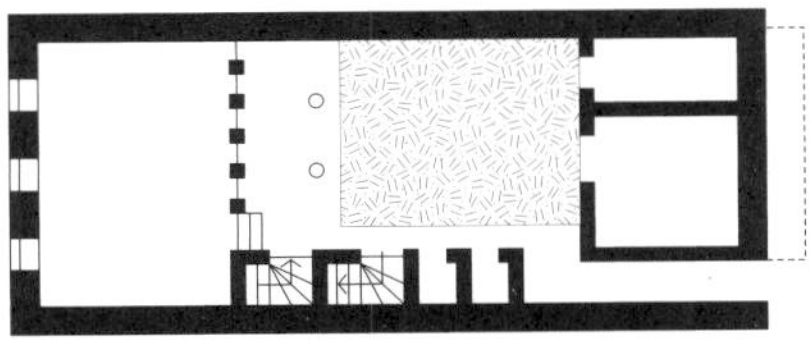

Ancient house, Egypt

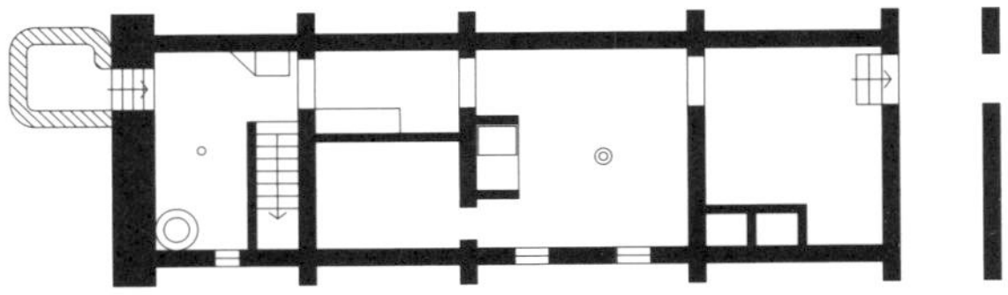

Examples of ground-floor plans of narrow
houses throughout history

30'

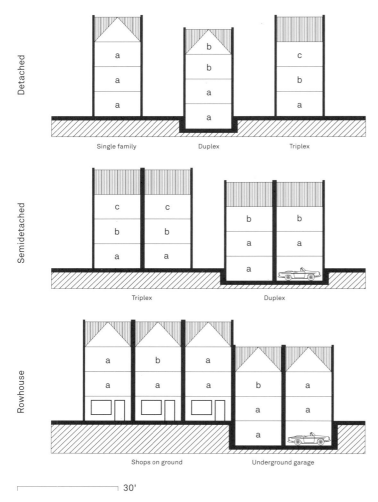

Single family      Duplex      Triplex

Triplex      Duplex

Shops on ground      Underground garage

30'

Possible spatial arrangements and attachment types

## Adhering to a Budget

Upheavals in the global economy have taken their toll on both the world markets and the lives of individuals. In past decades, buyers sought more expensive homes, some of which overstretched their financial limits. Meanwhile, secure employment and the steady incomes earned in traditional households began to diminish. Foreign competition in the labor market caused many low-paying jobs to be transferred overseas. Such recessionary cycles have affected work security. Young, first-time home buyers find it difficult to accumulate the means to purchase a home. One of the effects on the housing field has been that large-scale detached homes are now beyond the range of a growing number of potential buyers, and this has increased the demand for less-expensive smaller units.

Lowering a unit's cost can be realized by efficiently using all material and nonmaterial resources and simplifying the building's complexity. As mentioned earlier, the narrow house has compact qualities and unique economic advantages. The most noticeable savings begin with land and infrastructure costs. The joined units of rowhousing reduce lot areas and street lengths, and the configuration is one of the most effective ways of reducing energy consumption because heat loss is limited to fewer exterior walls and a smaller roof area. Joining four detached units into two semidetached dwellings, for instance, reduces the exposed wall area by 36 percent. Grouping all four houses in a row provides an additional 50 percent reduction. Heat-loss reductions of approximately 21 percent can be achieved when two dwellings are attached, and a further 36 percent savings for the middle unit can be achieved when three or more units are joined in a rowhouse formation. Grouping houses is also an effective way to improve construction efficiency. The repetition of parts usually results in a shorter construction period per dwelling, and the reduction in perimeter area can have a significant effect on delivery time, since constructing the envelope is labor-intensive and costly.

While grouping is not a defining feature of narrow housing, the rowhouse configuration is more apt to adopt a form, dimension, and overall geometry that is simpler and more economical. The common rectangular footprint of a rowhouse unit tends to allow for the most efficient and flexible interior layout. Vertical designs make the best use of space, because as density increases, the cost per unit decreases. Therefore attaching units serves an important role in achieving affordability. Placing them closer to the street saves the cost of extending the utilities. These advantages are discussed in later sections, where the various stages of dwelling design are examined in greater detail.

# Footprints & Volumes

In medieval Europe, taxes were levied in walled
cities according to the widths of street-facing
structures, forcing owners to limit the sizes of
building fronts. Location, architectural trends,
and technological innovation, among other
considerations, were also instrumental in the
conception of narrow-front housing. This section
focuses on large-scale issues affecting the design
of narrow dwellings. Siting, footprints, spatial
arrangements, attachment, access, facades,
and roof shapes, as well as use of outdoor space,
are among the subjects discussed here.

## Sites and the Environment

When a housing project is initiated, whether for a single unit or multiple dwellings, typically the site is chosen before a designer is hired. The objective is therefore to use it well. In addition to common challenges posed by the location, such as density and access roads, environmental concerns have taken center stage in recent years. Reducing the carbon (and physical) footprint, utilizing passive solar energy, and conserving local flora and fauna are some of the larger issues that designers need to concern themselves with, and these are addressed in the following sections.

When a detached dwelling is constructed on a large plot endowed with many natural features, the need to preserve or take advantage of what is there is of paramount importance. The trees should be evaluated to determine which are healthy or in need of pruning or removal. Trees that need to be protected (especially mature specimens) can be fenced or sectioned off. Guidelines suggest that a mature tree has a trunk circumference greater than 18 inches (45 centimeters) as measured from 40 inches (1 meter) above ground level. To prevent mechanical damage to the trunk, protection should be installed at a height of 60 inches (1.5 meters).

Before construction begins, the surrounding trees should be prepared with adequate pruning, watering, fertilizing, and root-system protection to avoid breakage caused by the disruption. To avoid damaging and depriving the roots of oxygen, the grade around each tree should not be altered, and barriers should be placed around the tree to prevent compaction of the soil.

Trees and shrubs catch and absorb stormwater runoff and prevent soil erosion. They also filter out noise and offer privacy and an appearance for all to enjoy. In the end, the trees should reflect the building orientation, height, setback, and fenestration. By keeping existing trees healthy on the site, proper environmental decisions are made more responsibly.

A site's original topography must also be preserved, because if altered it may not be possible to restore it, and this can forever change the local ecosystem. Native flora and other natural elements lend a site its distinctive character. Roads, driveways, and buildings can be placed to respect existing slopes and changes in elevation. Following these contour patterns can also prevent erosion.

Grading a site can also have negative impacts on the surrounding ecosystem. Erosion, for example, can disturb the site's natural drainage system and pollute nearby water sources. Less site disruption means a reduced flow of stormwater to nearby sources so that more water can be absorbed by plants. Maintaining the site conditions by constructing retaining walls, terraces, and other structures for stability will reduce the chances of soil erosion.

Exposure to the sun should also be considered when siting a dwelling unit to reduce energy consumption and increase access to natural light. The location and orientation of a building can maximize and capture solar energy year-round, especially during winter months. This issue is highly relevant in the design of narrow dwellings, since only two facades are exposed when units are built in a row. Daily and yearly positions of the sun can be evaluated during the initial planning stages by using sundials and solar path diagrams. Houses that are oriented toward the sun, with more fenestration on the sunny side, will catch the most intense rays in the early afternoon.

An alternative siting strategy takes into consideration the solar arcs created as the sun travels from east to west. Units oriented along the north-west axis (in the Northern Hemisphere) benefit from a shorter noonday shadow than might otherwise be cast for houses oriented along an east-west axis. Moreover, additional units may be erected at the edge of neighboring shadows if the dwelling design follows this layout. When considering sunlight and shadow orientation, it is important to avoid obstructions that will prevent surrounding houses from maximizing sunlight.

Existing natural vegetation and new growth can be used for shade. To minimize solar heat gain in summer, deciduous trees can be placed on the sunniest side of the house. The leaves of these trees shade the house from the heat but allow some light to penetrate indoors. In the wintertime, more solar heat and light can filter through the bare branches. Facades that are exposed to the sun with lesser intensity should be about 10 to 15 percent fenestrated. Maximizing the solar gain will lower energy consumption, which in turn reduces costs and the quantity of emissions necessary to produce this energy.

Another important aspect of environmentally conscious design is natural ventiliation. Trees and other vegetation play an important role in wind currents. Although patterns change from one season to the next, wind is determined by the landscape, time, and weather patterns. Its direction and speed can be evaluated for each area by looking at a wind square. For example, near bodies of water, the wind will blow from the direction of the water toward the land in the daytime, but it will reverse direction at night. As is commonly the case, the wind will flow around objects and keep the same direction of flow. As a result, nearby vegetation can greatly reduce wind speed. During cold months, trees act as shields from winter winds. Consequently, coniferous trees are appropriate winter wind blocks, as they maintain their foliage year-round. Their placement allows a house to benefit from summer breezes from the opposite direction of the winters winds. Favorable orientation will also allow for cross-ventilation, reducing the need for mechanical cooling. Siting issues are of concern to every housing project and more so for narrow dwellings. They are also important during the occupancy stage, when strategies to reduce energy consumption are implemented.

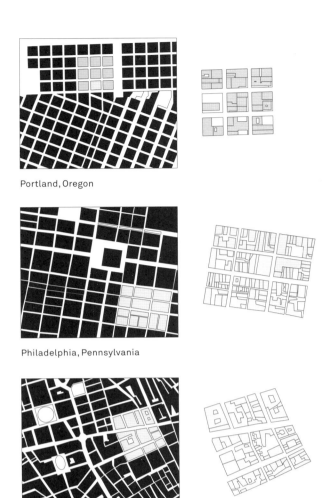

Portland, Oregon

Philadelphia, Pennsylvania

London, United Kingdom          ⌐ 500'          ⌐ 500'

Figure-ground diagrams demonstrating the relationship between block patterns and lot sizes for different cities

## Footprints

Urban settlement patterns and the length and depth of city blocks determined the proportions of existing narrow-front dwellings. Since European cities were built on the ruins of Roman towns, they adopted the Roman street patterns. From this configuration, a gridiron system emerged, one that over many centuries grew organically around the city center. Buildings following this pattern had their footprint set by the block's dimensions. The gridiron pattern later crossed over to the New World. Dimensions began to be regulated and were written into bylaws. A grid space of 500 to 660 feet (150 to 200 meters) was common and created a suitable network for pedestrian and vehicular movement. A typical block, with buildings at times touching each other's backs, was created, leaving only an alley for service access, ventilation, and light.

Common construction methods also influenced the widths of structures. Timber, a building material that was available throughout Europe, was used for both vertical and horizontal supports. Whenever possible, to increase interior flexibility, designers and builders tried to free up the space of bearing walls. As a result, they restricted the widths of buildings to the length of a typically available wooden log made into a beam. The beam rested on common walls, the dividers between adjacent structures, which at first were also constructed of wood; later, with the development of fire codes, these dividers were built of masonry. When other building technologies such as concrete and steel emerged, the dimensional limitations of wood disappeared.

The process and nature of a project's initiation and construction phases also affected its physical characteristics. Streets in the heart of an old city were often lined with narrow-front structures of an identical width. In other parts of the city, it was not uncommon for buildings to have a variety of widths. Large-scale projects by a single developer came much later. The Royal Circus (1754) in Bath, England, by architect John Wood I and The Hanover Terrace (1827) in Regent's Park, London, by architect John Nash featured a number of attached repetitive structures. In earlier centuries, however, privately initiated projects composed of many units were rare. An initiator would commonly purchase a plot on an empty block for a single building. Often a gap left between dwellings would be filled in years later. Since land was not always divided into identically sized plots, the widths of buildings also varied. Very small strips of land would, at times, be left for construction. Differences existed between rural and urban areas as well. In cities surrounded by defense walls, which had higher land costs and taxes, one can find narrower units. In small settlements and rural areas, the funding available to the builder was often the only determining factor.

A structure's footprint was also affected by rooms placed in lower and upper floors. In the absence of a cellar, the street level was either used as a place of commerce (primarily during the Middle Ages) or had a domestic function. The front room might have had a parlor, which was an early version of the living room, or a study with a view onto the street (during the Renaissance). It is common to find a hallway placed parallel to a front room, which often led to a rear staircase. A passageway stretching the length of the structure became a hallmark of narrow houses. The combined width hallway plus room ranged from between 12 and 18 feet (3.7 and 5.5 meters).

Upper levels were the occupants' private domain, and this is where the sleeping quarters were placed. The width of that level resulted from functions being placed next to each other. There could either be two bedrooms, a bedroom and a study, or a bedroom and a bathroom. The width of a bedroom, when one existed, measured approximately 12 feet (3.7 meters), matching the width of the floor below. The widths of structures were therefore affected by the second-floor layout.

The length of a narrow dwelling was set by functions placed along the longitudinal axis. On the lower level these included the parlor, stairs, dining area, and kitchen, and in later years a powder room. In upper levels there were primarily bedrooms, stairs, bathrooms, and at times a study. The minimum length of such a layout typically ranged, depending on the combination of functions, from 32 to 40 feet (10 to 12 meters). The lengths of units also affected the amount of natural light penetrating the house's core. Dwellings with very long footprints had interiors that, prior to the invention of artificial means of illumination, were dark and lacked ventilation. In several models, a central light and air well was constructed above the stairs and next to a bathroom.

## Arrangement of Floors

To maximize land use, narrow structures were several levels tall. The height was determined by the skills of the builders and the construction technology. In later years building codes limited the height for safety reasons, and quick exits were mandated for the occupants of upper levels, who needed to reach ground level in the event of a fire. Slender structures also relied on the physical support of adjacent buildings for stability and therefore could not extend to far above their neighbors.

The heights of narrow-front buildings were also determined by the presence of an underground level, which commonly served as a foundation. Roof shape, style, and use affected the building height, and inclusion of an attic, for example, made for a taller townhouse. The internal subdivision of the structure's levels was left, however, to the building's contractor. Some were built to house a single family, while others were divided among unrelated occupants. Narrow structures also acted as apartment buildings, housing several occupants on one floor. When the building was shared among several users, easy access to each unit was highly important. Allocating area to stairs in such a way as to not consume precious living space was of paramount importance.

It is also possible to vary the number of levels allocated to each occupant. A three-story structure can be designed to house one, two, or three households. Some contemporary builders divide them during the preconstruction phase based on the buyers' means and needs. A single user may purchase all three levels, or different levels can be sold to unrelated occupants to form a duplex or a triplex.

The chosen conceptual approach to the internal subdivision of volumes can also vary. In their 2008 book *Row Houses: A Housing Typology*, authors Günter Pfeifer, Per Brauneck, and Usch Engelmann classify narrow dwellings according to the interior circulation method, which can take several forms.

**A. Without staircase:** A single-story dwelling is perhaps the simplest form and can be designed with or without an inner courtyard.

**B. Longitudinal staircase:** The stair is located either along the party wall or in the middle of the space, in the long dimension.

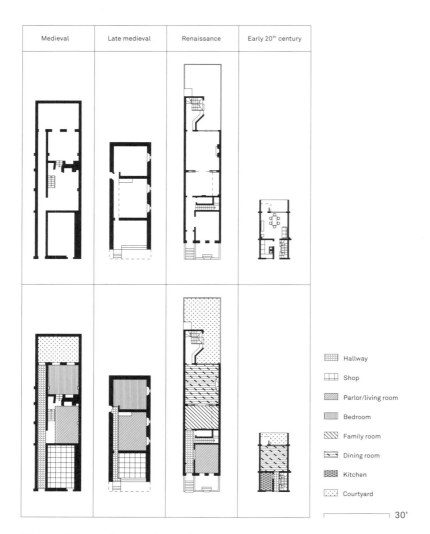

| Medieval | Late medieval | Renaissance | Early 20th century |
|---|---|---|---|

Legend:
- Hallway
- Shop
- Parlor/living room
- Bedroom
- Family room
- Dining room
- Kitchen
- Courtyard

30'

Analyses of ground-floor plans by function

Second floor

a. Master bedroom
b. Bathroom
c. Family room
d. Secondary bedroom

32'  36'  40'

Ground floor

a. Kitchen
b. Living room
c. Entrance
d. Dining room
e. Utilities
f. Powder room

32'  36'  40'

30'

Dimensional analyses of narrow-front dwellings with variable lengths

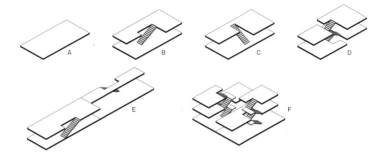

Layout options based on type of staircase and its position

**C. Transversal staircase:** This type requires a wider floor plan, since the stair is located perpendicular to the long wall.

**D. Longitudinal split-level:** The front and rear levels are split, with the stairs as the connecting element.

**E. Transversal split-level:** The floors can be broken into three sections in the long dimension, which creates a wide range of design possibilities.

**F. Back-to-back:** Fit for a dense urban design, the units are attached at the rear. An inner patio helps bring light into the core. Another version features two dwellings with a gap in between.

**G. Front-to-back:** This design reverses the front and rear of each dwelling. It is a variation of the back-to-back, with more sophisticated circulation.

## Attachments

As noted earlier, narrow dwellings can be constructed as detached, semidetached, or part of a row of several units. The architectural and urban ramifications of the chosen method of attachment are numerous, and it is worthwhile to list them here.

Starting with their legal titles, narrow dwellings can be owned freehold; that is, the occupants own the entire structure and the land on which it is constructed. They can also take the form of condominiums, in which each occupant, single or multifamily, owns the portion of the structure they occupy. The land, common walls, and roof are the shared property, toward which all residents contribute a monthly maintenance fee.

Condominium ownership offers a greater degree of flexibility and economy. One connection to infrastructure, water, and drainage systems, for example, is necessary for the entire row rather than separate connections. Some municipalities, however, place a limit on how narrow the structure's width can be. In others, when the width is less than a certain dimension, they can only be constructed as condominiums.

Another advantage of row housing is the savings on land and infrastructure costs. Simply put, the more units joined together, the greater the savings will be. Joining several structures to form a row

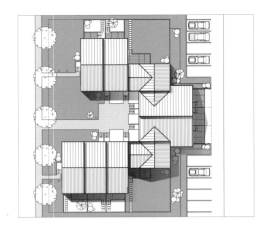

A cluster of narrow-front dwellings

results in a 33 percent savings of lot area and street length, and a 70 percent savings in the exterior wall perimeter. When designing row housing, the question arises as to the preferred number of attached units. Some European and North American cities have block-long rows of homes; however, residential developments with very long rows can often present a poor streetscape. The monotonous repetition of facades and cars parked in front has been known to be stigmatizing.

Options are available to break this monotony by varying the facade design or staggering the units, which can also contribute to greater front or rear privacy. When the units are staggered, however, the foundation and roof are likely to have more corners and be more complex, and therefore more costly to construct. Experience shows that joining between four and eight units, having facades no wider than 20 feet (6 meters) each, is suitable. The decision about how many units to join also depends on the number of stories, the type of roof, and the street width.

When considering the length and composition of the row, one possibility is to mix housing types. The end units in a row of six or eight buildings, for example, could consist of multifamily structures, whereas the middle units could be single-family homes. This would allow for a wider range of unit types and, as a result, target a broader range of households. Another type of row housing is the cluster, which is not built in a straight row. Clusters would likely be sold as condominiums, since large-size plots are needed, and the parking would be arranged in the common space.

When narrow structures form a row, the end units can be distinguished from the middle ones by placing the entrance and windows on the sidewalls. The front facades of these units, therefore, can have larger openings and more interior space.

Attached units can also provide the possibility for horizontal arrangements of spaces. A ground-floor unit (where zoning permits) can connect to an adjacent dwelling through the common wall, thereby offering a one-level unit without stairs for people with reduced mobility.

## Access and Egress

The main entrance to a narrow dwelling can be located in several places along the exterior. The most suitable location is in the front facade's extreme ends, which minimizes disruption of interior space and does not bisect the floor. Variations on this type include recessing or projecting the entrance to create a porch, which is especially suitable for houses that form a long row.

Other possible locations for a main entrance might be between the center and one of the dwelling's ends, which allows service functions or stairways to be placed on the smaller portion of the facade. A central entrance location works well if the structure is wide enough to have usable spaces on either side of the entryway. A front door's chosen location can also take into consideration the possible introduction of a second front door so that the structure can be converted into a multifamily dwelling. For example, placing the main door on one side of the front facade near a party wall leaves area on the other end for a second door if desired.

It is common to have a rear door as a secondary means of access or exit, for service or safety purposes, which is easier to accomplish when the house backs onto a lane. A carefully planned scheme that creates two main accesses to a dwelling occurs when the parking and the pedestrian path are on two different levels of a sloping site. This scheme allows for one entrance on the lower level from the parking place, and another on the upper floor.

## Ground Relation

Whether detached or attached, narrow dwellings can relate to the ground in various ways. The chosen design will depend on building tradition and desired architectural intention. Common in North America's colder areas, concrete, which is used for foundations, has a disadvantage as a building material: it cracks in temperatures below freezing under the pressure of expanding frozen soil. As a result, foundation walls have to be extended further below grade to where the soil's temperature is warmer. The depth of the footing on which the foundation wall rests depends on the altitude and

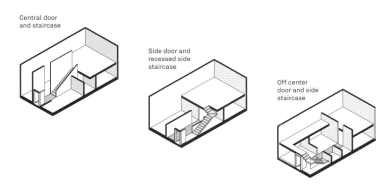

Possible placements for the main entrance and stairs

location of the building site. In Nordic climates, where there are more days with deep freeze temperatures, the foundation must be excavated lower. With the evolution of home construction, builders realized that when the soil within the perimeter of the foundation is removed, an entire floor, the basement, can be gained. This can be regarded as a "bonus space" and can take on a variety of roles, which will be elaborated below. When the ground slopes, the basement can be designed in the lower portion of the site, with entry level from an upper street.

When a basement is not required, the unit can be laid directly on the ground, also known as slab on grade. There are two types of slab foundations. The first, monolithic slab on grade, is designed so that the entire foundation is constructed in a single pour. In this design, the foundation's edge and the floor will be constructed at the same time.

The second, a frost-protected shallow foundation, is a variation of slab on grade. It is suitable for construction in cold regions and was designed to protect the foundation against freezing. This method is used primarily where excavating deep foundations is impossible. A shallow foundation can be constructed of poured concrete or concrete blocks. The challenge in laying foundations in cold regions is to prevent heaving, caused by the freeze-thaw cycle. Several methods are used to protect the foundation in such climates. Placing rigid foam insulation around the facing edges of the foundation is the most common. The same product is also placed around the perimeter of the structure below grade to a distance of 1 to 2 feet (0.3 to 0.6 meters).

The crawl-space foundation is another method of building a lower structural support for a home. It can be built using concrete blocks or poured-in-place concrete. The structure can be suspended on piers made either of wood or concrete. It is common to see such foundations in high-moisture areas. The lower floor is raised above ground, providing easy access to plumbing. The space between grade and the ground floor must be ventilated to prevent moisture from damaging the structure and to reduce the floor temperature. Crawl spaces also require attention to insulation since the plumbing may be exposed. The method commonly used in low-cost housing is to place insulation between the joists of the lower floor. Space needs to be left between the ground and the floor to allow for easy maneuvering. In such cases, vapor barriers are installed under the subfloor to prevent moisture leakage to the outside. Another method is to insulate the perimeter wall by affixing rigid insulation to the exterior or by installing batt insulation on the inside.

**Shape of the Roof**

Similar to a basement, the design of a roof may also be affected by regional factors. The style and articulation are often influenced by architectural traditions and climatic conditions. Regions with heavy snowfall or rain will likely have pitched roofs or flat roofs with a

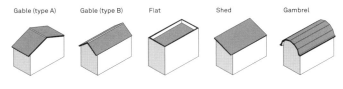

Gable (type A)  Gable (type B)  Flat  Shed  Gambrel

Roof types

superior drainage system. When poorly constructed, the roof can
be a source of heat loss. Proper attention to roof design can benefit
the space management of a narrow dwelling and provide means
for vertical expansion.

Until the middle of the twentieth century, roof construction was
a labor-intensive process. Carpenters constructed the roof on-site,
using solid-sawn lumber and low-cost labor, which resulted in
habitable roof styles. It was also an efficient way to manage the area
of a small home. The attic space, however, was an area of secondary
value. In affluent residences, the space was used for storage or as
the servant's sleeping quarters.

Along with other developments in home construction, the
method of building a roof has changed as well. The invention of
off-site prefabricated wood trusses has contributed significantly to
the reduction of labor and material costs. The attic space was also
reintroduced as an essential part of the space management of a
home. One of the best-known examples of such a design is the Cape
Cod cottage, where—with the absence of a basement—the attic
became an auxiliary yet useful family space.

Among the roof designs commonly used in North America,
the flat roof is fairly easy to construct. It is built much like another
floor in the dwelling. Joists are placed across the space and covered
with plywood and other roofing material. The development of space
trusses and I-joists, which rest on perimeter walls, eliminated the
need to construct bearing walls.

A flat roof can provide an area for future expansion, or it can
be used as a terrace for outdoor leisure activities. The design must
ensure that the existing structure will support another floor, a space
that could be easily accessed. When pitched roofs are designed,
attention should be given to their complexity. Intricate roofs will
not only take more time to assemble but, when poorly constructed,
they are also a potential source of heat loss. Furthermore, since heat
rises, a well-insulated roof will keep heat indoors.

A house's facade appearance is also determined by the roof.
Gabled roofs are one option; however, if the roof is pitched in
the narrow dimension and built in a row, there will be snow accu-
mulation between units, making this configuration unsuitable
in Nordic climates. A roof that slopes down toward the front
and rear may be appropriate for any climate. A shed roof is another
possibility, which allows for alternation of direction among
houses in rows, thereby creating a more interesting streetscape.

Depending on which type of roof is chosen, a variety of architectural details can be incorporated to enhance the dwelling's curb appeal. The inclusion of green roofs in residential designs has become more acceptable in recent years. For green roofs, the roof construction specifications need to be carefully considered and simple access to the roof provided.

### Facades

Narrow dwellings can be constructed in a variety of configurations. When built as detached or semidetached homes, the design will have a greater envelope area with which to work. There are more facades to cover and greater surface area for openings in a detached, narrow dwelling. The elevations also account for the building's energy performance. The choice between transparent and opaque, therefore, needs to be carefully made and consider the orientation and interior design. The need to let light into the structure's core has often led to the use of large glass-enclosed areas. The choice of other materials is influenced by style, location, and bylaws.

When proportions are considered, the need to work with narrow and tall shapes has led to the inclusion of similar dimensions when it comes to openings. Architects have often chosen to glaze the entire front and, at times, rear elevations in order to create spatial flow between interior and exterior. According to the local culture where the dwelling is located, balconies and decks can be included in either of the elevations to offer outdoor seating. The front and rear elevations may also include doors and parking garages, which take away part of the area allocated to windows.

The importance of a well considered facade is magnified, since the small width of a narrow house leaves less facade area, especially when adjoining a number of similar units. Architectural detailing can help instill a sense of place and permanence. Details such as railings, small overhangs at entrances, and window styles, for example, help to create a clear and identifiable character that enlivens repetition, regardless of width. Several strategies have been used to counteract the monotony often associated with this housing type, and these range from simple to complex. The easiest way to add character visually is through the choice of facade materials. Brick, for example, a material with timeless quality, comes in many patterns and colors; over the centuries, it has lent a pleasing effect to many cities. Wood siding is another vernacular option that, when painted in different shades, can produce a colorful setting.

In a large project, the architect can create a grammar and offer to the occupant a choice of facade features. For example, buyers may choose to have a front door with a porch, a balcony on the second floor, and a gabled roof. Their neighbors may choose to have a bay window on the first floor, two windows with no balcony on the second, and a flat roof. This mass-customization method not only creates more diverse and interesting neighborhoods but also enhances the occupants' sense of personalization.

Choice of facade components that can be offered to buyers in the preconstruction stage

Narrow houses are commonly used in infill projects, since most leftover urban lots are long and narrow. Therefore, it is possible to fit the house in with its established surroundings and draw from the architectural vocabulary of its neighbors. If the structure is located in a historic neighborhood, certain bylaws and guidelines may restrict the facade variations. Material choices and architectural details may be limited to the existing style. If the house is to be built in an upscale community, the great-house method of attachment is often the most appropriate. This strategy treats the facades of three or four attached units so that they resemble one large dwelling.

Construction practices of the building envelope have changed in recent years and continue to change to this day. Innovation has brought to the forefront new building products that reduce consumption of natural resources as well as save builders and buyers money. Some of these products have gained acceptance and are widely used, while others have encountered resistance. The two main products are engineered lumber and light-gauge steel. These manufactured products are used as joists, beams, and flooring materials. Glue-laminated lumber is actually stacked, finger-jointed layers of standard lumber. Another product is lami-nated-veneer lumber, which is made from thin layers of wood that have been glued together and run parallel to each other. Parallel-strand lumber, known as Parallam, is packed with long strips of wood fibers, which are glued parallel to each other. These products are more versatile than solid-sawn lumber, and their prices are becoming competitive and in some instances cheaper.

A product that shows promise but is not fully accepted by the home building industry is light-gauge steel. Steel studs offer several advantages: they have consistent quality; they do not rot, warp, or twist; they are fire-resistant and lightweight; and they are manufac-tured using recycled content. The disadvantage of the product is that many builders lack experience using it; consequently, there is a need to train the labor force in its use, as well as encourage consumer acceptance. Light-gauge steel studs are one alternative to wood and are likely to gain popularity in years to come.

Once the exterior studs have been constructed, insulation of the walls can begin. A wide range of products have been introduced over the years. The selection of products should be guided by the greatest energy-saving potential for the lowest investment. In general, batt insulation is the least expensive, yet it requires careful attention to proper installation procedures. Cellulose insulation, which is made of recycled newsprint, costs more than batt insulation and has labor-intensive application procedures as well, but it offers reduced air leakage and better sound insulation. Rigid foam sheets have higher R-values than other products, but they are known to be more expensive.

Heat losses through the building envelope can occur by any of the following three processes: conduction, convection, and radiation. In all three cases, windows are the weakest link in the thermal performance of the envelope and, as such, represent the most important investment in the construction or renovation of any dwelling. They are also highly variable in price, appearance, and performance, making their selection a difficult process.

Generally, windows with fewer operable parts are less costly and more energy efficient. The longer the joint, the greater the potential for heat loss through leakage; therefore, fixed windows are best in this regard. As for operable windows, pivoting components are more energy efficient, since they make use of compression seals. Sliding parts are least effective in terms of air leakage. The general quality and craftsmanship of a window are also critical. A poorly assembled casement window from one manufacturer, for instance, can be susceptible to more air leakage than a well-crafted sliding unit from another. A poor seal can overcome the advantages of using a casement or awning window.

## Prefabrication

Their small width makes narrow dwellings suitable for prefabrication. Constructing a structure in a factory and transporting it to a site for assembly is becoming more and more common. In fact, mobile homes are built this way and shipped to customers across North America. There are three main prefabrication methods.

A. **Modular construction:** Factory fabrication of sections that can consist of an entire house or part of one. The sections are sent to the site where they are hoisted into place by crane.

B. **Kit of parts:** Well-marked building products, such as studs or windows, that are shipped to the site for assembly.

C. **Panelization:** Panels of different sizes, some with framing only and others with insulation and windows, are assembled according to plans.

As is the case with any manufactured component, waste generated by prefabrication of panel systems is less than what could be expected from on-site construction. Assembly of the wall system in closed, controlled environments ensures that materials are used efficiently, and offcut pieces of material are more easily recovered and reused. Furthermore, the fact that the home is erected and closed to the elements within a short period of time reduces construction delays due to bad weather. Considering that the construction of an average house produces 5,512 pounds (2.5 metric tons) of waste—25 percent of which is dimensional lumber and an additional 15 percent is manufactured wood products—cost savings could be substantial, particularly in large developments.

When considering the time saved by using either modular or panelized prefabricated systems, there is an additional advantage. Due to the quick and efficient assembly that takes place on-site, the effects of poor weather conditions, particularly in colder climates, is reduced, as is the potential for damage due to inadequate material storage and vandalism. Construction management and trade coordination can be simplified, and the need for large teams of skilled labor for multiple-unit construction is substantially lowered.

## Parking

The need to house a car can pose a challenge to designers of narrow dwellings. When a detached unit is built on a large plot, there are fewer constraints or limitations. An independent indoor garage may be constructed or an outdoor spot found. The situation may be different, however, when the home is part of a row. Since bylaws in most jurisdictions mandate on-lot parking of at least one vehicle, the solutions are to park the car either indoors or outdoors in a relatively small area.

Avoiding long walks, guarding against theft, and keeping vehicles warm on cold days are the prime reasons given by residents for wanting to park next to home. Indoor parking is known to cost significantly more than an outdoor spot. In addition to allocating valuable space inside the building, driveways must be prepared. The visual effect that parking has on a street is also an important consideration. Additional challenges include how to place the car inside a small structure and the fact that garage doors lining the lower level of rowhousing harm a street's appearance.

There are several effective ways, however, to park cars indoors without jeopardizing the streetscape or building a separate parking structure: shared indoor parking. With this model, a concrete slab is built on top of a basement level, under a row of detached or attached homes. There are a limited number of access points to the parking floor, from which homeowners can enter their units. The space can be subdivided into separate garages or remain undivided and open. Joint parking solutions can also occur under the end units of a row, on the surface or underground. The end unit may not have a basement or a lower floor, but the street's appearance will benefit by not having a row of imposing garages. A design can also be introduced whereby the cars have access to an individual basement garage from the rear. The back balconies in these homes can be suspended over an entryway to the parking. In exchange for indoor parking, an occupant would not have a traditional backyard. The access roads to these arrangements can all be shared with neighboring units. Sharing access roads can economize land in small-lot housing and reduce the number of curb cuts, thereby creating continuous sidewalks.

When outdoor parking solutions are considered, shared common areas are one option. A parking lot located a long distance from homes will not be appreciated by people carrying heavy loads. Providing drop-off places in front of a dwelling, after which the car can be driven to a parking area, could be an acceptable compromise. A maximum recommended distance between the home and a parking area is 150 feet (45 meters). The distance should be reduced for senior citizens and can be increased when the path is covered.

Parking areas can also be designated as play areas, but the designer needs to focus on slowing traffic by introducing speed bumps or changing the road-paving material. Visitor parking is another key concern in high-density housing. Bylaws require the allocation of parking places for visitors. It is common to see visitor parking located further away from the dwelling, giving priority to occupants. In such a case, a drop-off should be planned to provide easy access for a visiting elderly or disabled person. In cul-de-sac configurations, visitors' parking can be part of the road.

Another suitable outdoor parking solution for a row of narrow dwellings is an alley or laneway. This passageway, in the middle of an urban block, runs behind homes and has been part of the evolution of Eastern and Western cities' urban history. Alleys have gained popularity in recent years and are used in neotraditional developments. Lanes contribute to a reduction of lot width by permitting the garage to be at the rear of the house. Narrow lots served by rear lanes result in significant land savings of up to 50 percent compared to developments with 50-foot (15-meter) lots.

Lanes can provide several parking alternatives for narrow dwellings. Cars can be parked outdoors in individual lots or in group arrangements. Parking can also take place in a garage built off of the laneway. Alternatively, residents can park in the dwelling itself, with rear or side entry.

## Outdoor Areas

Much like parking spaces, outdoor areas of narrow dwellings also offer a challenge. Whereas freestanding units on large lots do not pose such a problem, spaces in and around high-density rowhousing need careful attention. A designer needs to consider solutions within the dwelling by using courts, balconies, and decks.

Ground-level exterior areas function best as extensions of indoor living spaces when attached to the living room or kitchen.

Having a kitchen window that looks onto the enclosed outdoor space provides an opportunity for supervised children's play. At times, the outdoor living space, which acts as an extension of the dwelling itself, may not be completely enclosed for privacy. It is recommended that the size of the space have a minimum area of 600 square feet (54 square meters) for privacy reasons.

In dwelling units without direct access to the ground level (such as triplexes) decks or balconies can serve as private outdoor spaces and connect directly to the home's living areas. For one-bedroom units, balconies should be at least 6 feet (1.8 meters) deep and have a minimum area of 65 square feet (6 square meters). Ideally, balconies should be recessed into the building to create a sense of privacy, and a minimum of 60 feet (18 meters) should separate facing balconies with no other means of visual screening.

While private outdoor spaces tend to be located at the back, the front yard space, however small, serves an important communal function. It acts as a transition between the public and the private realms and defines the owner's identity. In the front yard residents can plant trees to create privacy or place a flower bed.

As far as communal space is concerned, neighborhood parks are to be shared and enjoyed by all; while smaller communal areas can form a more private setting for small clusters of dwellings. One of the best contributing aspects of the design of such spaces is the height-to-width ratio, which can define the space and affect its level of privacy and intimacy. In medium- to high-density housing units, this common space typically has a height-to-width ratio between 1:5 and 1:3. For example, in a project with housing clusters that are 30 feet (9 meters) high, the common space in between clusters should measure approximately 90 to 180 feet (27 to 54 meters) across. Communal areas for clusters of homes help create semiprivate areas for residents and reduce the need for large private yards for individual units. Generally, the smaller the private area for individual dwellings, the larger the communal area should be.

# Interiors

Limited widths pose several challenges
to designers of narrow-front dwellings, since
several rooms need to fit within a relatively
small area. The integration of natural light,
especially for middle units in a rowhouse
configuration, is another difficulty. Over the
centuries, innovative strategies have been
developed to cope with these constraints.
This chapter explores the interior spaces of
a narrow house. The topics discussed include
space distribution, circulation, privacy,
and flexibility, among others.

## Typologies and Principles

Various approaches to the overall interior design of narrow dwellings have been suggested over the years. They are commonly the outcome of cultural attitudes, trends, and of course, whether the dwelling is attached or detached. Designers of traditional dwellings tended to enclose and separate the different functions from one another. The dining room, for example, was formal, with its own proportions and door. This organization was relaxed in the twentieth century and replaced by the open plan, which saw rooms merged into one another with no partitions. This approach was reflected in the combination of living, dining, and kitchen spaces that were merged into one large area. The sleeping area, on the other hand, remarkably resembles similar spaces in traditional dwellings. Each bedroom is enclosed, although a loft-type design can be found in which an entire level, with the exception of the plumbing fixtures, is left open.

When homes are built in a row, exposure to natural light is critical. Ideally, each function may have an exposure to daylight, but this is often not possible and prioritization needs to occur. The tendency is to locate the kitchen and the living room in each of the dwelling's extremes, and, on the sleeping level, to place the bedrooms at either end. On both levels, the center is occupied by utility and service functions, into which penetration of natural light is less important.

When designing a small dwelling, function and perception of the space must also be addressed. Without this combination, the design will not be successful. A boat, for example, is an extremely efficient and functional small space, but few people would want to reside on a boat for a long period of time. The huge, two-story entries in many new suburban homes, on the other hand, inspire a sense of spaciousness but serve no real function and are frequently described as wasted space.

By marrying efficiency with a sense of space, one can design narrow homes that feel comfortable and personal rather than cramped and suffocating. Designers of compact economy cars, for example, found a way to combine spaciousness and functionality. By carefully considering the driver's ergonomics and maneuverability, they were able to inspire a sense of space, despite the car's small dimensions. Being attentive to detail and treating space as a precious commodity can encourage good design.

When focusing on space efficiency, it is important to study lifestyles and how people use homes. By reviewing which spaces are important and used most, some less-used areas can be eliminated altogether. Creating multifunctional spaces can greatly reduce the floor area of a dwelling while still fulfilling the occupants' functional needs. By reducing interior walls, a designer can achieve practical and alternative means of dividing spaces, such as shelving units that free up space and create more opportunities for storage.

Optimizing the storage potential of a small space can also help reduce unnecessary floor space, eliminating the need for a basement or excessive closets.

Creating a sense of space is also essential to the success and appeal of small dwellings. Careful selection of floor material, colors, window size and placement, ceiling height, and floor plan orientation can help produce the desired spatial effect in a home. Before discussing specific space-saving and perception-enhancing strategies for small dwellings, it will be worthwhile to examine the home and identify ways of increasing large-scale functionality.

## Movements

The design of narrow dwellings requires careful attention to movement through the floors and the location of stairs. In general, reducing the amount of space allocated to circulation is the objective. The designer is likely to try to assign most of the area to the functions themselves. The common approach would be to use the less-lit areas for movement, which in townhouses would be the axis along the longitudinal wall. Another approach in the living area is to move through the spaces themselves, which is not recommended, as it creates an interior design challenge. Other influential factors would be the location of the stairs and their chosen shape.

Despite a house's small width, there are a number of possibilities for locating a stair and designing circulation. On occasion, different staircase types may be combined to respond to the layouts of different floors. For functional reasons, the stairs are typically located at either the front or middle of an entrance level. It is practical to place the stairs near the entrance for fast and easy access to upper levels. A rear location is undesirable, since it is far from the entrance and would block natural light. The location of the stair and its chosen type determine the layouts of upper or lower levels. Reaching the middle of the sleeping floor or the attic would be preferred, since it would free the extreme ends for bedrooms. This would be less of a priority in a basement floor, when it exists, where arrangement of functions is less formal.

There are a variety of staircase types that work well in narrow dwellings. A simple model is the straight run, which for a central location in an attached dwelling can be placed along one party wall, at the front of the house near the entrance or further down the wall. When the stair is in the middle, it is usually surrounded by spaces that require plumbing, such as the kitchen and bathroom. A variation on a straight run stair consists of adding a spiral stair to the upper levels, thereby minimizing the use of floor area.

Another commonly used stair is the L-shape, which can be placed in a variety of locations. The ninety-degree turn allows designers to tuck this stair into corners. It is usually placed close to the entrance. Turns at the beginning and end forms a U-shaped stair, and when there is a central void, an atrium can be created. When a skylight is placed on top, natural light flows down.

A U-shaped staircase can expand to encircle the perimeter of the house, creating a large uninterrupted core. Another consideration is the makeup, design, and appearance of the stairs. In a small house, stairs can easily be turned into an attractive architectural feature. Their chosen materials and style plays a critical role in making the space airy. Leaving the stairs open by removing the risers or using cantilevered thin treads are approaches used in some designs. Treating the handrail similarly can further contribute to lowering the stair's visual impact on a small space.

Regardless of where the stairs are in a house, there are a few circulation options on each floor. The path may be literal, with walls creating hallways and corridors, or implied by furniture arrangement in an open plan. Circulation paths may also be pushed along the party wall to form a single-loaded corridor, or centrally placed to form a double-loaded corridor. Placing the path slightly off-center provides room on the smaller side of the divided space for stairs, storage, services, and utilities, while in the center it tends to create two extremely narrow spaces (on either side of the corridor) that are too small to be functional. When the width of the house permits, however, the stairs, storage, services, and utilities may be located all along one side.

## Space Distribution and Room Arrangement

The distribution of rooms in narrow houses depends on, among other considerations, the site, building codes, inclusion of an indoor garage, architectural trends, and cultural norms. The lower level, whether a basement or ground floor, will often be devoted to utilities, the second to living spaces, and the upper to sleeping. When the site is sloped, it is also common to see bedrooms on ground floors, with living space above.

Various rooms within a home are organized into several classifications of zones. Public, semipublic, and private spaces are one zone-designation method. Public areas consist of the living and dining rooms, which can be used by the occupants and their guests. Semipublic areas include spaces such as the kitchen and bathrooms, while the bedrooms are private. Another way of zoning functions is to divide them into day and night, depending on their time of use. Day functions are often public or semipublic areas, such as the living room and kitchen, while night spaces include private functions, like bedrooms. Alternatively, spaces may be zoned according to their function, such as living, sleeping, or service areas. There can be many possible room arrangements within a given narrow dwelling unit, often grouped according to common space divisions. Description and analysis of these spaces is provided in the following sections.

### Entrance

For many, the process of entering a home begins with a front porch and the path or stairs leading up to it. Despite their small size in narrow dwellings, porches or covered stoops give visitors a sense of arrival and designate a specific point of entry. They also provide shelter from the rain as homeowners unlock the door and visitors wait to be received. Additionally, the front porch or stoop creates an intermediary zone between the street and the home—an outdoor room that eases the transition.

Once inside, the entryway becomes a homeowner's and visitor's first impression. It can also serve a variety of functions that greatly increase a home's space efficiency. An entryway must be large enough to permit at least two or three people to stand and talk comfortably. In cold regions, where a second indoor entry door is often provided, the closet can be placed in between to save space. Ideally, the view from the entryway will offer interesting images as well. In long homes, such as rowhouses, this view should extend the length of the interior, preferably with an opening at the far wall.

In certain designs, when there is no basement, the ground floor may house the garage and utilities. It is also possible to find a guest suite, study, or home office at the rear of this level. In such cases, the dwellings' living area is on the second floor, reached easily by stairs. In some regions, there is commonly a powder room a short distance away from the entrance, preferably located discretely for privacy.

*Living Room*

Locating the living room will largely depend on the best view and the quality of light. When facing south the room enjoys plenty of sun. The location also depends on whether the building is attached or detached. For a freestanding unit, side walls can be glazed to offer a view of the site. When located as a middle dwelling in a row configuration, the options are often limited to the front or rear.

For narrow interiors a variety of strategies can be employed to make spaces feel larger. Although not commonly thought of, the careful manipulation of ceiling heights can help to designate different spaces for different activities and make certain areas look wider than they really are. In designs that use an open plan, varying floor and ceiling heights is an effective method for dividing spaces without building walls and sacrificing valuable floor area. Low ceiling heights foster a sense of warmth and privacy, making them work well for bedrooms and alcoves. Having a small space, such as a hallway or kitchen, with a lower ceiling that opens into an area with a relatively high ceiling enhances its sense of spaciousness. An entrance with a low ceiling, for example, that looks into a living room with a taller ceiling will foster openness upon entering.

One way to create the illusion of a tall ceiling without incurring additional construction costs is to leave the ceiling joists exposed. The voids between them create the illusion of a taller space, while adding character. Sound transmission can be a problem with exposed joists, however, as less material exists between floors to absorb noise.

### Dining Room

In nineteenth-century designs, a formal dining room was common. After World War II, changing lifestyles led to casual eating in the kitchen, which is currently used as the household's social area. When space is at a premium, the rarely used formal dining room is not included in a narrow-front layout. Alternatively, the dining room becomes part of the living room or an extendable kitchen table can accommodate occupants and guests when needed. When more interior space is desired, exterior bay projections may provide an additional dining area. When a narrow house is detached or an end unit of a row, the projections are likely to be on the house's longitudinal side. In the middle unit of a row, projections are limited to front or back. When the unit is particularly long, a formal, well-defined dining room with its own door can be created. In contemporary design one often sees movable screens for partitioning off dining and living areas.

### Kitchen

A variety of kitchen locations and configurations can be used in narrow dwellings. The linear kitchen is highly compact and therefore a good fit. A small one can occupy an area of 35 square feet (3.3 square meters), and a medium-sized one may be 91 square feet (8.5 square meters). A U-shaped kitchen also has a suitable layout, with an area of 48 square feet (4.5 square meters). The galley kitchen consists of appliances and a counter set parallel, with an area of approximately 65 square feet (6 square meters). L-shaped kitchens are another option, with areas comparable to galley kitchens. Islands are occasionally used, but they are less common, since they take up more space.

When a kitchen is centrally located, it can act as a divider for separating living and dining areas. It can also be located at either end of a floor, leaving the remainder open, as a combination of living and dining spaces. Alternatively, a line kitchen may be placed

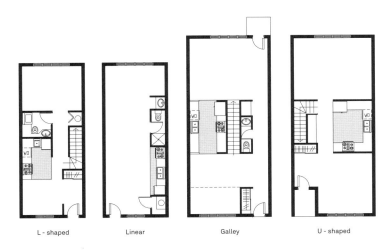

L - shaped        Linear        Galley        U - shaped

Kitchen locations and their varying typologies        30'

Possible arrangements of bedrooms based on narrow-front widths of
14, 16, and 18 feet (4.3, 4.9, and 5.5 meters)

along one party wall, minimizing the space it occupies. When the kitchen is not on the same level as the living or dining rooms, it is often on the lowest floor, which follows a design of older narrow-front-style homes.

Contemporary interior designs have turned the kitchen into a distinct visual feature. The use of stainless steel counters and appliances, as well as appropriately designed lighting, help make the space both a display and a gathering space. No longer tucked into the rear, the kitchen is an area to show off.

### Bedrooms

The dimensions of bedrooms in a narrow dwelling can vary widely, since their sizes are partially determined by the available space and the number needed. The master bedroom, however, is often the largest, occupying the full width of a floor. En-suite bathrooms and walk-in closets may be included, which provide a sense of larger space. Smaller secondary bedrooms have their own closets and a shared bathroom.

The placement of bedrooms depends on light, views, noise, and privacy; therefore, they are commonly located on the top floor. In a one-story house, when the bedrooms are on the same floor as the living spaces, they are usually sited at the rear, away from the entrance and separated from the living areas by the kitchen, stairs, or utilities. Regardless of whether the bedrooms are on the upper or lower levels, the floor is naturally less open in plan and has only a small hallway or limited circulation space. Balconies are often attached to bedrooms to form outdoor living areas. Glazed balcony doors will make a small bedroom feel larger.

### Utilities and Storage

When designing the utility and service spaces in a narrow dwelling, it is best to begin by understanding the plumbing network. Ideally, these functions may be placed on top of each other to shorten utility lines. A well-located water supply and drainage can free up space for other functions.

The placement of storage and utilities conduits often depends on the desired location of the spaces that require plumbing. When the kitchen, for example, is located in the center of a floor, there are two common configurations for storage and utilities. The first is to place the kitchen, closet, and utilities in a central core, with circulation on either or one side. Alternatively, the kitchen, storage, and utilities can be separated to create a passageway in between. When the kitchen is located along the party wall, it is common to see utilities and storage components along the same wall. The powder room or even the upper-floor bathroom is often part of this core.

A spatial requirement that has resulted from a contemporary lifestyle is the need for additional storage. Due to the lack of space, creating adequate storage areas in a narrow house can be challenging. Common methods include closets, outdoor sheds, and built-in units. Other necessary locations for storage are near the entrance (for coats and shoes) and in bedrooms. Under-stair storage is creative and a highly efficient use of leftover space. Hallways can also be used for storage if properly designed. A corridor width of 48 inches (120 centimeters) permits 12 inches (30 centimeters) for shallow closets or shelves. Outside-storage lockers and sheds are also typical and can be located on a rear porch or at the very front.

*Residual Spaces*

Residual spaces are leftover areas after all of the rooms and circulation areas have been allocated. In larger homes, these spaces are less important, but in narrow houses—where space is at a premium— they can be exploited and used. In addition, the creative use of residual spaces can help with everyday domestic chores and even give a home its unique character.

The area under the stairs can be considered a residual space that can be used in a variety of ways. A drawer built into the stair, for example, can provide storage for everyday items. For stairs next to a living room, the lowered ceiling area under the stairs can define a work space and create the impression of a distinct place for a specific activity. For stairs beside a kitchen, the space can be enclosed to serve as a pantry. An alcove is another pocket of space used to separate one activity from the main room. It can be created by suspending a bay over the side of the home.

The best strategy for utilizing residual spaces is the creative use of areas not commonly thought of as valuable. One such approach can be assigning multiple uses to the very same space. A counter, for example, can unfold from the wall to become a desk, and it can be folded back to add more area to the living room. A window seat is another type of alcove that consists of a bench area, with a view of the exterior. To optimize its use, the area under the bench's seat can provide extra storage.

Basements and attics can also be considered a type of residual space. Measures should be taken to ensure that basements can support a variety of functions. By raising the ceiling of the basement above grade, windows can introduce natural light, making the space suitable for a bedroom or family room. Basements can also be used as indoor parking garages, with entrances from the front or rear.

Planning for the future, through indoor expansion, was the focus of the Grow Home, which I designed in collaboration with several colleagues as a demonstration unit. The basement was left unfinished for the occupants to complete themselves or with a hired contractor at a later date. The dwelling's footprint, which measured 14 by 36 feet (4.3 by 11 meters), provided approximately 500 square feet (46 square meters) at the basement level, permitting a variety of interior configurations in the narrow, unpartitioned space. When the Grow Home was later built by developers, most buyers purchased the unit with an unfinished basement and completed it progressively. They created a variety of layouts that suited their household needs and budget. A postoccupancy study of two hundred dwellings showed that 25 percent of all the occupants built family rooms, 23 percent chose to create a laundry space, 21 percent used the area for more storage, 13 percent built bedrooms, and the remaining households built for other functions.

Using the basement as a livable space provides an opportunity to create an independent, accessory dwelling unit. The unit may have its own entrance and be used as a source of supplementary income for the household above. Such a solution would be possible in neighborhoods where multifamily units are permitted. A similar objective can be achieved when the basement becomes a home office with an independent entrance or access through an upper floor.

When an attic is designed to be habitable, similar to a basement, it can be left unfinished. Regardless of its state of completion, some key features need to be provided to accommodate livability. Windows should be installed in advance, based on the preplanned floor layout. These can be regular windows placed on the roof's gable ends, a dormer in the front or the rear of the dwelling, or both. A fixed or operable skylight can also be installed to let in light and fresh air. When energy efficiency is a chief consideration, it is best to avoid installation of skylights and dormers, since they are likely to be a main source of heat loss.

### Views

Since narrow-front rowhouses have a small footprint, neighbors can potentially be closer to one another than in detached dwellings. Therefore, the designer needs to be concerned with privacy, without decreasing natural light and restricting views to the outside. Several design strategies can help achieve these goals.

Since attached narrow houses only have two fenestrated facades, reducing the amount of glazed area for privacy reasons is not an option because it would significantly reduce the amount of natural light. Using frosted glass is one method to provide ample light while achieving privacy. Alternatively, carefully locating windows can ensure that enough sunlight enters without giving neighbors a view inside.

There are a number of design decisions that can help increase indoor privacy as well. Narrow-front townhouses do not have space to waste on large entry foyers or halls. Therefore it is common to enter directly into a room, rather than into a vestibule. Locating a less-private space, such as a study, at the front of the unit eases the transition from public to private. Placing the most private areas, such as the bedrooms, at the rear or on the upper levels also helps maintain the occupants' privacy. If the views outward are better from the upper floors, the living spaces rather than the bedrooms may be placed there. This arrangement can also provide more privacy to the occupants, since it is more difficult for neighbors to view the upper floors compared with the lower ones.

## Flexibility

Despite the narrow width, different degrees of interior flexibility and adaptability can be achieved by using a variety of design strategies. These encompass a wide range of interpretations, but share the same principle: fitting occupants' spatial needs within the dimensional constraints of their homes. Ease of interior modification therefore extends the life of the house, reduces waste, and eliminates unnecessary moves.

In an open plan, rather than partitioning and creating spaces suitable for one use only, the interior can be kept free of partitions. Living and dining rooms may be placed wherever one desires. At a later date, occupants may choose to alter their locations. At an even later date, a partition may be built to create a separate space, another bedroom, or a home office. By initially keeping the floor plan open, changes made over the passage of time involve building rather than tearing down.

Strategies for future adaptability also include the structure. When interior partitions are non-load-bearing, structural supports are limited to the two long walls; therefore, any future reconfigurations are possible. Many changes can be made without concern for the house's structural integrity. Also the structure may be designed to withstand additional loads. An entire floor may be added, increasing its size and potential use, with minor alterations to the floors and structure below. Contemporary construction methods and products have made it easier to use design strategies that permit adaptability.

## Space Efficiency

In addition to utilizing a home's residual spaces, various materials and products can also increase the efficient use of small areas and add to the overall sense of spaciousness. Such strategies also lend themselves to adaptability, as they can be easily altered without the need for demolition or construction. Pocket doors provide desired privacy to an area and take up less space than traditional swinging doors. While a traditional swinging door requires clearance that restricts the placement of furniture, pocket doors, once opened, hide completely within the wall cavity. Pocket doors are best suited for areas that remain connected but where occasional separation is desired, such as between kitchens and dining rooms.

To keep costs low, homes can be constructed and sold with only a few enclosed rooms. As a family grows and changes, however, additional partitioning may become necessary. With the current methods of constructing partition walls, such changes are expensive and will cause great disruption to a homeowner's daily life. Walls that have been developed for use in office buildings, however, offer easy installation and relocation. At present, prefabricated walls are code-approved for commercial use and permitted for residential use only in certain jurisdictions.

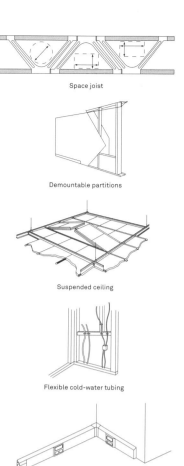

Space joist

Demountable partitions

Suspended ceiling

Flexible cold-water tubing

Floor molding

Construction products that ease interior adaptability

There are three basic types of wall systems. The first is a mobile or operable system, which has a sliding mechanism that allows a wall panel to move along ceiling tracks. The second type is a demountable system, similar in concept to the traditional drywall system. Walls are constructed with metal studs that are placed at specific intervals. Prefinished gypsum wallboards are then affixed with special clips to the metal frame. The third type is the portable partition system, made of prefabricated panels, which are brought to a desired location and held in place by channels in the ceiling and floor.

Another option for creating interior partitions is by using sliding screens. This space-dividing method is common in Japan, where large screens made from wooden frames and paper are moved along tracks affixed to the floor and ceiling. In Western homes, where floor tracks are uncommon, similar screens can be developed with tracks in the ceiling. Sliding screens can be thought of as large doors that help create spaces without taking up large amounts of floor area. While such screens provide useful visual dividers, sound is still transmitted through them, so they should not be used for areas that require acoustic isolation.

Furniture partitions work in several ways to increase the efficiency and comfort of small homes. Using shelving and furniture to divide spaces reduces the need for interior partition walls. Additionally, furniture partitions help make small spaces feel larger by blurring boundaries between rooms and by allowing the eye to see beyond them, preventing small spaces from feeling boxed in. When shelves, cabinets, or other storage units are used to create partitions, small areas are provided with much-needed storage space. Furniture partitions also make spaces versatile, as they can be moved easily to change the size and function of spaces.

The tendency, when designing homes with a small floor area, is to see their interior design as a challenge. The measures listed above demonstrate that various steps can make narrow dwellings feel spacious.

# Historical Chronology

One must investigate the urban and architectural roots of narrow-front homes to better understand their design. The building type, with its many variations, has flourished on several continents, but Western Europe and North America will be featured here because they offer the most relevant examples. Since much of the documented history refers to rowhousing or townhouses, this section deals primarily with these types. The chapter is organized chronologically, beginning with the medieval period and ending with present times. Each segment examines relevant changes in urban planning, living habits, and cultural trends affecting design and construction.

## The Middle Ages

Street patterns are far more telling of a city's evolution than the sum of its individual houses. This is especially true of medieval Europe, where narrow-front rowhouses were born out of regulations in landownership and were intrinsically related to the organization of roads. Under the Roman Empire, converse town planning proliferated across Europe. The gridiron, a pattern in which streets cross each other perpendicularly, was used in most cities of classical antiquity, from the Mediterranean region of the Greco-Roman world to the Orient, and it could be applied to virtually any site. Its simplicity also made it highly flexible. While it did not inherently consider a specific landscape, it was easily adaptable and synthesized with other planning models. The most common form of the system was applied to land that was extensive and plain.[1]

The gridiron street system is exemplary in the medieval town of Ragusa, better known today as Dubrovnik, located at the southern tip of Croatia on the coast of the Adriatic Sea. Toward the end of the thirteenth century, the settlement prospered with trade, and it grew. Streets were laid out according to the gridiron system, with north-south and east-west orientations.

In 1292, a fire raged across the town, resulting in a reconstruction effort in which the streets were paved and widened. Another outcome of the fire was a more uniform relationship between landowners and residents. The geometric nature of the street system ensured an even distribution of land, since it was easy to attach an appropriate price according to variations in lot sizes—an important factor to equitable rent. The plots, therefore, became narrow to maximize income. These parcels of land were divided by size and degree of uniformity, and they were leased annually. Because towns required efficient land use, it was in the best interest of the landlord to restrict the frontal width to between 13 and 25 feet (4 and 8 meters). Leasable area could only be gained by increasing depth; therefore, the plots became long and narrow. Within the town, the most extreme cases were found on broad streets that accommodated markets. Encroachment onto the street was common, and corner sites had the added benefit of a doubling of the street facade.[2]

As far as the structures themselves were concerned, few remnants of Roman culture existed in the floor plan of the typical house. One of the exceptions, however, was the emphasis on designating separate rooms for specific daily activities, which determined a general layout pattern and organization. Roman-English residences further integrated the essence of this pattern in future designs.[3] A design innovation specific to the Middle Ages, however, was the *undercroft*, a room underneath a building for storage. These rooms measured approximately 50 by 20 feet (15 by 6 meters) and were dug 6.6 feet (2 meters) belowground to provide sufficient storage space. By the year 1100, undercrofts were lined with stone and built on ground level as well. Despite the cost, stone remained the primary material for these structures until the advent of brick. Even with the threat of

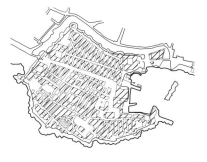

Urban plan of Dubrovnik, a medieval fortress city on the Adriatic Sea

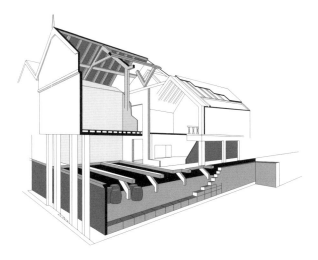

Section drawing illustrating an undercroft in a building in the Rows,
Chester, England, built ca. 1725

flooding, undercrofts provided a firm and level base for the structure
above. A decorated entrance to the space was a social status symbol
and was commonly used by merchants as adjunct to their homes.[4]

Shops and covered galleries are also recognized as features of
medieval towns. Undercrofts allowed the ground level to be reserved
for commercial activities. Even the most modest towns had thriving
markets along streets that extended from the gates of castles or
monasteries. These elements have been best preserved in the Rows in
Chester, England, which developed in response the site's conditions.[5]

Surviving medieval narrow-front rows existed as continuous
entities along streets, not as sparsely located singular buildings.
These dwellings remain significant as an exemplary synthesis
of Roman urban planning principles and vernacular developments,
namely the development of undercrofts that permitted the coexist-
ence of commercial and residential uses.

### The Renaissance

The Black Death that struck Europe in the fourteenth century
eliminated a third of the population, regardless of an individual's
location or social status. It also had strong repercussions on religious
institutions. Slowly, secular despots assumed power and sought
to eliminate all traces of the medieval period. Nevertheless, relief from
overcrowded cities was only temporary, as the population caught up
to the pre-epidemic count and continued to grow, pressuring the city
to expand its boundaries. A complete rebuilding of the fortification
walls was out of the question and would lead any city to bankruptcy.
Solutions were therefore directed internally and necessitated the
densification of the city with taller buildings.[6]

Taller and more densely populated towns did not imply chaos;
rather, the power shift into secular hands made greater clarification
and order possible during the building process. This was guided by

a set of planning principles implemented in the growing city. The entangled streets were widened and made straight to enhance vistas. Squares were also better appreciated as public centers and reinforced with groupings of residences built in rows.[7]

The centralization of monarchical power, symbolically manifest in the reconfigured town, was consistent with the tendency among nobility to emulate the "fashionable." While circumstances bid the nobles to reside in townhouses, they were designed to emulate the looks and atmosphere of elaborate palaces. An increased number of servants in the house affected its layout and organization. Narrow-front townhouses evolved to be perceived as primarily domestic dwellings and completely detached from the mixed-use connotations of its medieval forms, which facilitated standardization. By this time period, narrow-front townhouses were considered a refined, generic building type for the masses.

Double bay windows and an entry door composed the front facade of a typical narrow-front townhouse of this era. The ground floor was connected to the street by a couple of steps, providing entrance through a vestibule. The parlor was located at the front on the ground floor; it was the first room that one would enter. Beyond the parlor, the dining room had a view of the backyard. This was the most convenient place for dining, because it was directly above the kitchen and service rooms. Underneath the ground floor were, typically, a partial basement and cellar resulting from the lowering of the ground as the house receded from the street after years of road surface accretion. The second floor, or *piano nobile*, had especially high ceilings and contained two parlors: one in the front for men and one at the rear for women. The third floor contained master and children's bedrooms. Finally, the *garret* was the upper level occupied by servants.[8]

While the layout of narrow-front row homes was more or less generic, the aesthetic appearance was variable, as it was an important tool for attracting occupants. This is most evident along the city of Amsterdam's four major canals, which were lined with around 2,200 houses. On the ground floor of these buildings, a small set of steps, called a *stoop*, would later be adopted in New York City (called New Amsterdam in the seventeenth century). Stairs were given added width to create a more luxurious indoor appearance. Spacious outdoor gardens were incorporated behind these houses, which were restricted to a maximum of 100 feet (30 meters). Interior courtyards had to be placed within the house to ensure sufficient lighting.[9]

Timber was the most common material for constructing narrow-front townhouses, but in England after the Great Fire of London in 1666, timber construction was seen as a fire hazard. Furthermore, there were not enough trees to reconstruct London using timber, which would have increased the nation's dependence on imported softwood from Northern Europe. Stone was seen as a fire-resistant and durable material. Brick also became abundant as a cheap, premanufactured product.[10] Because homes were also places of

Fourth floor

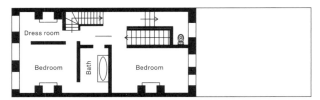

Third floor

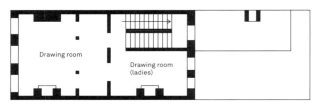

Second floor

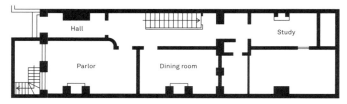

Ground floor

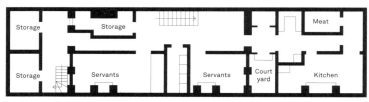

Basement

30'

Floor plans of a typical narrow-front townhouse in the
Renaissance period

business for some residents, there was evidence of extra precautions for security. Not only were there dangers of robbery, there was fear of riots from low-paid weavers. Many houses therefore installed exterior bars and shutters on ground-floor windows.

In summary, narrow-front homes built during the Renaissance were distinct from those of the Middle Ages. Most significant was the fact that they became more attractive and suitable to the upper class.

## The Neoclassical Age

In England, the typical Georgian terrace house consisted of between four and six stories, in which all domestic activities, including eating, sleeping, and entertaining company, as well as the kitchen and servants' quarters, were accommodated on distinct floors. When affordable, an extra floor added more luxury and comfort to the dwelling. Naturally, narrow-front townhouses were assessed according to their respective numbers of stories. The Great Fire of London in 1666 led to a series of building acts that brought uniformity and introduced strict construction methods. In the London Building Act of 1667, row houses were classified into four different rates primarily determined by a dwelling's width and height.

There were a variety of possible layouts in the floor plan of an English narrow-front townhouse. The one-room floor plan reflected a special concern for maximizing daylight and had little to do with the economy of ground space.[11] The one-room plan represented a conscious decision to accept the discomfort of stairs in a vertically arranged house, which was likened to "a bird perched inside a cage."[12] The two-room plan involved different placement of the chimney and staircase. A central chimney stack was used in early examples, as it was perceived to be the cheapest option. This was followed by the central staircase becoming a more suitable option for narrow-front houses with incorporated commercial properties. This was an especially popular model among the poor. Finally, the rear staircase plan became a typical layout after the Great Fire, because it provided a privacy buffer between the homeowner and servants; however, as land prices increased, the central-staircase layout remained the most affordable option.[13]

By the eighteenth century, England was being built in the Palladian style, in contrast to the rococo-embellished structures of much of the rest of Europe.[14] The marginal popularity of elegant simplicity on one continent was compensated for on another. In parts of North America that were under England's colonial rule, the earliest builders were still familiar with the construction methodologies of European cities. The classical English terrace house was the natural choice and became the main pattern of domestic architecture. One of the most notable changes to the design of townhouses when they reached North America was that they became typical housing for the moderate and relatively poor populations. Substandard construction of narrow-front townhouses found its way across the Atlantic, and the emerging cities of America were just as vulnerable to chaos as their European

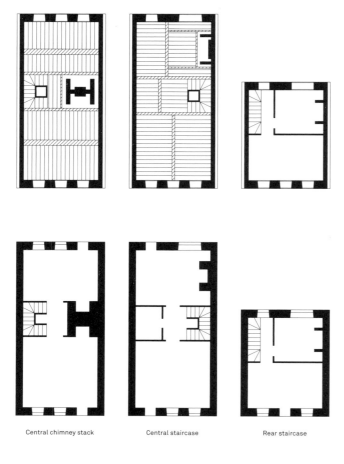

Central chimney stack      Central staircase      Rear staircase

30'

Floor plans from Stephen Primatt's *The City and Country Purchaser and Builder* (1667), with central chimney stack, central staircase, and rear staircase configurations.

precedents. Narrow-front homes in the North End of colonial Boston were a mixture of houses inspired by vernacular language and others that followed academic ideas. The Paul Revere House (1680), for example, has urban characteristics by virtue of being situated in the North End, but it also features a provincial vocabulary in its decorations.[15]

Indeed, these stylistic choices reflected conventions in decoration such as street facade, trims, and fireplace walls, but they were not the essence of debate, which centered on architectural alternatives to the floor plan. In fact, common builders were occupied with generating a diverse selection of interior arrangements, while keeping a more standardized external appearance to best accommodate the "middling sort." Often, they simply borrowed from existing narrow-front homes in England. In the mid-Atlantic cities, like Philadelphia, the central-staircase plan, which allowed for a shop on the front

30'

Floor plans of typical narrow-front townhouses in the Federal style,
built primarily in New York City, 1830s

half of the ground floor, dominated streetscapes. Occasionally, in
place of an internal corridor leading to the staircase, there were
external passages that branched off from the streets. The central-
staircase plan divided the house into two vertical segments and could
also house front and back tenements, if needed. It also made for a
more unnatural transition from one floor to the next, allowing greater
privacy. Many Philadelphia townhouses had back buildings that
housed servants, carriages, and workrooms.[16]

In New York after the American Revolutionary War ended in 1783,
the city's population was half of what it was in 1775. The number
of inhabitants quickly recovered, tripling within ten years. New York
became a magnet for people and a prosperous port for shipping
facilities. Fueled by this wealth, the city's population continued to
increase and a new building boom began.[17] During these years, the
Federal style was the prevailing motif until the 1830s.

As New York had, in essence, no regional style, it was a transitory departure from the Georgian style into the various classical revival styles of the 1830s, '40s, and '50s. These revivals were not an attempt to copy the ancient styles but were the result of a search for the essential principles applicable to all forms of architecture.[18]

The entry doorway was given considerable attention as a public display. Front facades were commonly embellished with lintels over doors and windows. Modest houses followed a pattern of two stories above the high basement, with a pitched roof and two dormers. In the 1820s, the rowhouse was typically wider, and no deeper than two rooms for the sake of having adequate sunlight, making the house better suited to the human scale. This new spatial ratio implied that the rear room on the first floor, too small for the dining room, be relocated to the front room of the basement, adjacent to the kitchen. Needless to say, this arrangement was especially favorable for the servants, as it simplified the frequent walks between the kitchen and dining room. Time spent eating two or three meals a day in the basement was more informal than before. Low ceilings, measuring 6.5 to 7 feet (2 to 2.1 meters) were common, which must have made the kitchen hot during the summer. With time, the basement was given greater height by deeper excavation, rather than by adding more steps to the first floor. There were no cellars inside the house; food was stored underneath the ground-level garden, where the natural coolness was suitable for storage. In later decades the garden was leveled to the floor of the basement. The kitchen, bedrooms, dormers, and family dining room were all subordinate in embellishment compared to the entrance facade and formal first-floor parlors.[19]

In the late seventeenth century to early nineteenth century, narrow-front American homes were stylistically attached to their English and Dutch roots. Nevertheless, there was dynamism in architectural design that continued into the next era, bringing further changes.

## Eclecticism

After years of copying English architectural handbooks, nineteenth-century America began questioning the relevance of these traditions within the culture of a newly independent nation. The decline of the Federal style was followed by the rise of the Greek Revival style for the next several decades. As with the many revival styles that would follow, the resulting buildings tended to make churches, banks, and residences indistinguishable from one another despite their differences. There was a self-conscious intent to stimulate the emotions by evoking an association with a distant time and place. This intent was born of the Romantic idea that "forms were beautiful for the emotions they evoked."[20] But this idea resulted mostly from an obsession with the culture of historical context, following the internationally publicized excavations of ancient Rome and Greece, which captured the interest of many. Therefore, it should be of no surprise that there is little distinction between the appearances of

Elevation facades of Colonnade Row, also known as La Grange Terrace, New York City, designed by Seth Geer, Architect, 1833

the Federal and Greek Revival styles. Generally, houses following the Greek Revival style were distinguished by their recognizable columns and ironwork. The proportions were taller. Instead of having two floors plus a dormer, these houses had a complete third floor and the roof was shallow, making it barely visible from the street. [21]

The Gothic Revival style, which came later, was never as popular in New York as it was in the rest of the United States during the 1850s and 1860s, but it played a crucial role in the refinement of the architectural ideals laid out by the Romantic movement. The problem was mostly poor execution; Gothic-inspired elements seemed to appear, whereas everything else was Greek Revival or Italianate. For example, the favor for asymmetry in Gothic architecture was absent in the plan, as it remained essentially the same as the classical style. Instead, Gothic elements were expressed through exaggerated architectural ornamentation that seemed to disturb the simplicity and calmness typically sought inside a home. The introduction of machinery to produce such ornamentation aggravated the situation into a monstrous absurdity. Thus, even at the time, there was general agreement that Gothic Revival was hardly appropriate for an urban environment, or that its use should be confined to sacred structures, such as churches.[22] The preference for dark-colored materials made brownstone, once again, the preferred building material.

During this era the most significant change was the declining engagement of small-scale builders and craftsmanship. The streetscape became more homogenous, as narrow-front row after row was mass-produced. This stirred nostalgia for rural life, and many people began to reassess life in the city.

## Modern Era and Contemporary Times

After World War II, planners brought forth designs that had both the convenience of urbanity and relaxation of rural life, with the intent of making the model community. The ideals of cities were strictly intended to move away from narrow-front homes. The very word "urban" became associated with the most squalid conditions of the city and stripped of all previous connotations of splendor and luxury. Just as earlier advances facilitated the mass production of row housing, new technologies were applied to the production of detached houses. With the advent of the affordable car, public transit was no longer a prerequisite for community planning. Designing for automobile traffic became more important.[23]

In the first half of the twentieth century, only a handful of famous architects dabbled in narrow-front house design. Le Corbusier had an irreconcilably contradictory but crucial influence on town housing. In his famous book *Five Points of the New Architecture* (1926), he outlined new principles of design, including horizontal windows, rooftop gardens, and the *plan libre*.[24] Most importantly, his designs celebrated the arrival of the automobile.

Another notable architect, Bruno Taut, was a key figure in the housing developments of postwar Germany. In a project near Berlin, he and several other architects took on a housing development of ten thousand dwellings.[25] The project was an ideal model, sensitive to the provision of community facilities and the propriety of the *Reihenhaus* or rowhouse. He believed that houses situated on an appropriate layout were more conducive to the community than large apartment blocks.

Like their European counterparts, North American developers were apprehensive and shared similar concerns. Row housing had to be reconfigured in response to competing suburban developments. With plummeting demand for narrow-front homes, cities like Baltimore saw their last construction of luxurious rowhouses in 1910. Disguised under the name Group Homes, alternative housing was placed in the suburbs for the wealthy, who wanted neither the responsibility of maintaining a large garden nor a city apartment. Not only did these homes provide variety, they also served to insulate the expensive inner lots from the less-expensive surrounding homes.

Daylight Rows were also of interest as upscale Group Homes. While sufficient light was always a major concern for narrow-front rowhouses, this was the first time it was used as a marketing scheme. It was one of the markers signifying the incorporation of suburban ideals into the row design. Recorded as 20 feet wide and 36 feet deep (6 by 11 meters), shallowness was the strategy for allowing daylight and fresh air to reach all of the main rooms of the seven-room house. These Daylight Rows were placed at the ends of streetcar lines, near the old city boundaries of Baltimore.[26] Private automobiles were placed in back of the rows, sometimes in an existing garage. They were built in the Italianate style, which was not an easy endeavor considering the shortage of building material during World War I.

Narrow-front rowhouses during the four decades from 1910 to 1950 were almost exclusively built for the poor. These efforts were concentrated on re-creating communities after the disasters of war,

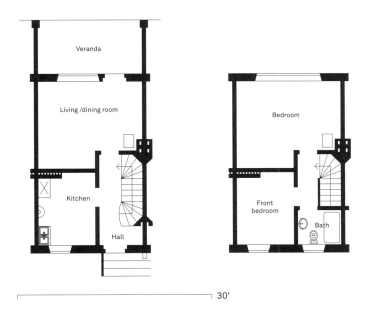

Veranda

Living /dining room

Kitchen

Hall

Bedroom

Front bedroom

Bath

30'

Ground- and first-floor plans of Type II House, designed by Bruno Taut and built in Berlin, Germany, 1925–27

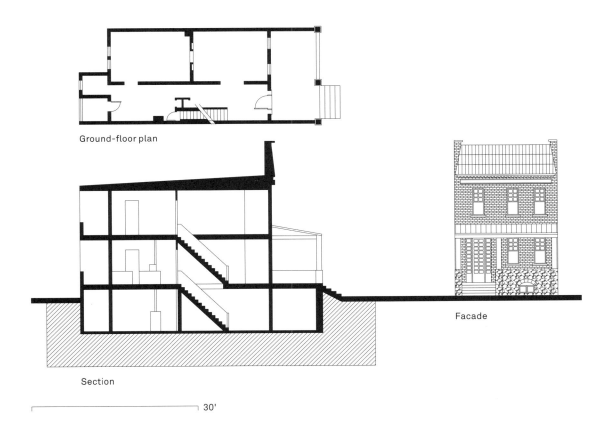

Ground-floor plan

Section

Facade

30'

The Daylight Rows, built in Baltimore from 1915 onward, were advertised as "a city house with suburban advantages."

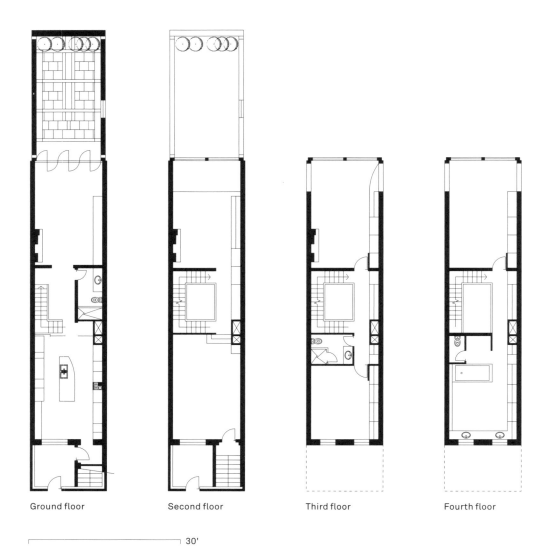

Ground floor          Second floor          Third floor          Fourth floor

⊢————————————————————⊣ 30'

Plans of the Hilpert House, designed by Ogawa/Depardon Architects,
New York, New York, 1998

but without satisfying any Romantic ideals, including access to the outdoors for healthfulness.

Once narrow-front homes were being designed for higher living standards, comparable to those of the suburbs, townhouses were rejuvenated and dissociated from the negative connotations of city life. This time, new elements were incorporated into the design. One of the most obvious was space for car storage. With the majority of families owning a car by the 1950s, it soon became common for a family to own a second car.[27] The contemporary version of the rowhouse was designed for middle-income families.

The layout of contemporary narrow-front houses seems to enable more freedom of personalization than ever before. The conventional arrangement of rooms is typically reconfigured to take advantage of surrounding views, and most homeowners are open to reintroducing office space inside the house.[28] Postwar designers and builders experienced a high demand for housing. They had to incorporate efficient and economical construction strategies. Extraneous decoration and ornamentation were the first elements to go. This freed up wall space, allowing windows to cover a greater area. Instead of the inward focus of the old home, the new home is based on looking outward from inside. As compensation for the decreased floor area, residents borrow exterior space.

Contemporary housing has followed a series of room reorganizations. Greater presence of domestic activities within the house is inevitable. The kitchen has been liberated from the back room. In some cases sliding partitions are the only boundaries that distinguish the bedroom from the living room so that the bedroom can become an extension of the living room when more space is required.

Some of the new developments in narrow-front homes involve complete renovations, such as the Hilpert House in New York (1998), designed by Ogawa/Depardon Architects.[29] In this project, steel and glass make the house glow in brilliant contrast to the neighboring townhouses. With the use of lofts and closets attached to only one side of the wall, the plan brings maximum openness.

## Notes

1.  Anthony Quiney, *Town Houses of Medieval Britain* (New Haven: Yale University Press, 2003), 83.
2.  Ibid., 87–88.
3.  Ibid., 133.
4.  Ibid., 146–7.
5.  Ibid., 151–2.
6.  Norbert Schoenauer, *6,000 Years of Housing*, vol. 3, *The Occidental Urban House* (New York and London: Garland STPM Press, 1981), 138–9.
7.  Ibid., 141.
8.  Ibid., 169.
9.  Marcus Binney, *Town Houses: Urban Houses from 1200 to the Present Day* (New York: Whitney Library of Design, 1998), 46.
10. Quiney, *Town Houses of Medieval Britain*, 253.
11. Kevin D. Murphy, *The American Townhouse* (New York: Harry N. Abrams, Inc., 2005), 36–37.
12. Peter Guillery, *The Small House in Eighteenth-Century London: A Social and Architectural History* (New Haven: Yale University Press in association with English Heritage for the Paul Mellon Centre for Studies in British Art, 2004), 41.
13. Murphy, *The American Townhouse*, 37.
14. Binney, *Town Houses*, 80.
15. Bernard L. Herman, Town House: Architecture and Material Life in the Early American City, 1780–1830 (Chapel Hill, NC: University of North Carolina Press, published for Omohundro Institute of Early American History and Culture, 2005), 8–9.
16. Ibid., 3–4.
17. Charles Lockwood, *Bricks and Brownstone: The New York Rowhouse, 1783–1929* (New York: Rizzoli, 2003), 1.
18. Ibid., 7.
19. Ibid., 11–19.
20. Ibid., 56.
21. Murphy, *The American Townhouse*, 23.
22. Ibid., 99.
23. Mary Ellen Hayward and Charles Belfoure, *The Baltimore Rowhouse* (New York: Princeton Architectural Press, 1999), 149.
24. Alexander Gorlin, *The New American Town House* (New York: Rizzoli, 1999), 16.
25. Binney, *Town Houses*, 11, 138.
26. Hayward and Belfoure, *The Baltimore Rowhouse*, 130–2.
27. Schoenauer, *6,000 Years of Housing*, 259.
28. Ibid., 259.
29. Gorlin, *The New American Town House*, 68–77.

# BIBLIOGRAPHY

Arendt, Randall G. *Conservation Design for Subdivisions.* Washington DC: Island Press, 1996.

Binney, Marcus. *Town Houses: Urban Houses from 1200 to the Present Day.* New York: Whitney Library of Design, 1998.

Fisette, Paul, and Dennis Ryan. "Preserving Trees During Construction." http://bct.nrc.umass.edu/index.php/publications/by-title/preserving-trees-during-construction/.

Friedman, Avi. *The Grow Home.* Montreal and Kingston: McGill-Queen's University Press, 2001.

Friedman, Avi. *Sustainable Residential Development: Planning and Design for Green Neighborhoods.* New York: McGraw-Hill Professional, 2007.

Gorlin, Alexander. *The New American Town House.* New York: Rizzoli, 1999.

Guillery, Peter. *The Small House in Eighteenth-Century London: A Social and Architectural History.* New Haven: Yale University Press in association with English Heritage for the Paul Mellon Centre for Studies in British Art, 2004.

Hayward, Mary Ellen, and Charles Belfoure. *The Baltimore rowhouse.* New York: Princeton Architectural Press, 1999.

Herman, Bernard L. *Town House: Architecture and Material Life in the Early American City, 1780–1830.* Chapel Hill: University of North Carolina Press, published for Omohundro Institute of Early American History and Culture, 2005.

Lamontagne, Jean, and Diane Brazeau. *Entretien et taille des jeunes arbres au Québec.* Saint-Laurent: Québec, Éditions du Trécarré, 1996.

Le Corbusier. *Vers une architecture.* France: Getty Research Institute, 1923.

Lockwood, Charles. *Bricks and Brownstone: The New York Rowhouse, 1783–1929.* New York: Rizzoli, 2003.

Mayer, Peter W., and William DeOreo. *Residential End Uses of Water.* Denver, CO: American Water Works Association, 1999.

Murphy, Kevin D. *The American Townhouse.* New York: Harry N. Abrams, Inc., 2005.

Nebraska Energy Office. "Minimizing the Use of Lumber Products in Residential Construction." http://www.neo.state.ne.us/home_const/factsheets/min_use_lumber.htm.

Organization for Economic Co-Operation and Development (OECD). *Motor Vehicle Pollution: Reduction Strategies Beyond 2010.* Paris: OECD Publishing, 1995.

Pfeifer, Gunter, and Per Brauneck. *Row Houses: A Housing Typology.* Basel, Switzerland: Birkhauser Verlag AG, 2008.

Quiney, Anthony. *Town houses of Medieval Britain.* New Haven: Yale University Press, 2003.

Schoenauer, Norbert. *6,000 Years of Housing.* 3 vols. New York and London: Garland STPM Press, 1981.

**Biagi House**
Architect: David Biagi, Architect
Principal designer: David Biagi
Designers: J. Quintin Biagi Sr. and J. Quintin Biagi Jr.

**Borneo Sporenburg**
Architect: KCAP Architects & Planners
Principal designer: Han van den Born
Designers: Hiltje Huizenga, Rik Houtman, Arend-Jan
    Burgwal, Tanja ten Berge, and Ingrid van Ommen

**Chameleon House**
Design: Anderson Anderson Architecture
Principal designers: Mark Anderson, AIA and Peter
    Anderson, FAIA
Designers: Brent Sumida and Hannah Brown
Consultants: Terry Nettles, PE/SE, Comstock
    Construction Company

**Eight Terraced Houses**
Architect: Enrique Mínguez Martínez, Architect
Principal designers: Enrique Mínguez Martínez and
    Antonio López Sánchez
Designer: Jesús Garcia Fuentes

**Fitch/O'Rourke Residence**
Architect: Robert M. Gurney, Architects
Project designers: Robert M. Gurney, FAIA and Hito
    Martinez
Interior designer: Therese Baron Gurney, ASID
Structural engineer: D. Anthony Beale, LLC
Mechanical engineer: Brian Ford

**Galley House**
Architect: Donald Chong Studio
Principal designer: Donald Chong
Designers: Chris Routley and Sandy McIntosh)
Contractor: Derek Nicholson
Structural engineer: Blackwell Bowick Partnership
Mechanical consultant: Thomas Technical
Geotechnical engineer: Haddad Geotechnical
Landscape design: Red Twig Design
Interiors and lighting: Karen White

Kitchen cabinetry: Bulthaup
Custom millwork: Daniel Thompson
Miscellaneous metals: George Pietras
Custom metal fabrication: Etmeco Ltd.

**Glass Shutter House**
Architect: Shigeru Ban Architects
Principal designer: Shigeru Ban
Designers: Nobutaka Hiraga and Keita Sugai
Structural engineer: Shuichi Hoshino, Hoshino
    Architect & Engineer
Mechanical engineer: Chiku Engineering Consultants
General contractors: Heisei Construction

**Harless Residence**
Architect: Dean Nota Architect
Principal designer: Dean Nota, AIA
Designers: Robert Sweet and Joseph Fedorowich

**Heran House**
Architect: Caan Architecten
Principal designers: Carla Degryse Koen Heijse and
    Wim Lahousse
Designers: Wim Heylen, Roel Cocquyt, Thomas De
    Keyser, Marijn Vanhoutte, Tom Declercq, Charlotte
    Dereu, and Christophe Gardin
Engineer: Jos Coene

**Holly Barn**
Architect: Knox Bhavan Architects
Address: 75 Bushey Hill Road, London, SE5 8QQ,
    United Kingdom
Principal designers: Simon Knox and Mary Lou Arscott
Designers: Sasha Bhavan and Lucy Thomas
Structural engineer: Eckersley O'Callaghan
Contractor: Willow Builders Ltd.
Joinery: Riverside Joinery
Landscape designer: Buckley Design Associates

**House MS**
Architect: Martiat Durnez, Architectes
Address: Rue Saint-Remy, 17, 4000, Liège, Belgium
Principal designers: S. Durnez and Fx Martiat
Designer: I. Clauwers
Engineer: Etudes Techniques SPRL

**Laneway House**
Architect: Shim-Sutcliffe Architects
Principal designers: Bridget Shim and Howard
 Sutcliffe
Presentation drawings: Donald Chong
Structural engineer: Ned Onen, Onen & Hayta
Mechanical engineer: Frank Toews
Builder: Chris Miller, Ptarmigan Construction
Color consultant: Margaret Priest
Landscape consultant: Neil Turnbull

**Modern Wooden Town**
Architect: Tuomo Siitonen Architects
Principal designer: Tuomo Siitonen
Designers: Freja Ståhlberg-Aalto and Tommi Lehtonen
Structural engineer: Gabrielsson &
 Pietiläinen Oy

**Outeiro House**
Architect: Ezzo
Principal designer: César Machado Moreira
Designers: Fátima Barroso and Pedro Almeida
Structural and services engineer: Oval

**Pine Forest Cabin**
Architect: Cutler Anderson Architects
Principal designer: Jim Cutler, FAIA
Designers: Bruce Anderson, AIA, Russ Hamlet, Joe
 Hurley, and David Cinamon, AIA
Structural engineer: Monte Clark Engineering
Contractor: Bjornsen Construction

**Salt Point House**
Architect: Thomas Phifer and Partners
Address: 180 Varick Street, 11th Floor,
 New York, New York 10014, United States
Principal designer: Thomas Phifer
Designers: Greg Reaves, Christoph Timm, Jonathan
 Benner, Joseph Sevene, Inoko, Kerim Demirkan,
 Katie Bennett, and Matthew Jull

**S.H.**
Architect: Katsuhiro Miyamoto & Associates
Principal designer: Katsuhiro Miyamoto
Designers: Takeshi Shakushiro, Miho Tsujioka, and
 Takashi Murakami

**Suisse Option Home**
Architect: Bauart Architekten und Planer AG
Principal designers: Willi Frei, Stefan Graf, Peter
 C. Jakob, Emmanuel Rey, Yorick Ringeisen, and
 Marco Ryter
Sales: WeberHaus GmbH
Wood contractor: Wey Elementbau AG, Villmergen

**Slice House**
Architect: Procter-Rihl
Principal designer: Christopher Procter and
 Fernando Rihl
Collaborators: Dirk Anderson, James Backwell, and
 Johannes Lobbert
Structural engineer (glass and steel): Michael Baigent
 MBOK
Structural engineer (concrete): Antonio Pasquali
Foundation engineer: Vitor Pasin
Services engineer: Flavio Mainardi
Site architect: Arq. Mauro Medeiros

**Sliding House**
Architect: MacKay-Lyons Sweetapple Architects
    Limited
Principal designer: Brian MacKay-Lyons
Designers: Talbot Sweetapple, Jesse Hindle, Tony
    Patterson, and Peter Broughton
Engineers: Campbell Comeau Engineering Ltd

**Slit House**
Architect: AZL Atelier Zhanglei
Principal designer: Zhang Lei
Designers: Lu Yuan and Tang Xiaoxin

**T Residence**
Architect: Studio Rinaldi
Address: 21 Chester Row, London SW1W 9JF,
    United Kingdom
Principle designer: Stephania Rinaldi
Engineer/architect of record: Elie Geiger, PE,
    Geiger Engineering, PC
Landscape design: Paula Hayes, principal

**Townhouse in DC**
Architect: Robert M. Gurney, Architects
Principal designers: Robert M. Gurney, FAIA and
    John Riordan
Engineer: D. Anthony Beale, LLC
General contractor: Prill Construction

**VH R-10 gHouse**
Architect: Darren Petrucci
Principal designer: Darren Petrucci
Engineer: Sourati Engineering Group
Landscape consultant: Renata Hejduk
General contractor: Darren Petrucci

**Webster Residence**
Architect: Ehrlich Architects
Principal designer: Steven Ehrlich, FAIA
Designers: James Schmidt, AIA, George Elian,
    and Justin Brechtel
Landscape architect: Jay Griffith

**Wohnhaus Willimann-Lötscher**
Architect: Bearth & Deplazes Architekten AG
Principal designers: Valentin Bearth, Andrea Deplazes,
    Daniel Ladner, and Bettina Werner
Designer: Tamara Bonzi
Engineers: Jürg Buchli, Haldenstein/Holzforum,
    Ostermundigen
Building physicist: Edy Toscano AG
Building services: Pius Monn, Ilanz/Vinzens AG

**Wohnpark am Betzenberg**
Architect: AV1 Architekten Butz Dujmovic Schanné Urig
Principal designers: Jürgen Butz, Boris Dujmovic,
    and Michael Schanné

# IMAGE CREDITS

## Detached Dwellings

Sliding House / p. 18 bottom left, by Brian Mackay-Lyons; all others by Greg Richardson; all photographs © MacKay-Lyons Sweetapple Architects Limited

Holly Barn / All photographs, Dennis Gilbert-View

Biagi House / All photographs, David Biagi

House MS / pp. 33, 35 bottom right, and 37 top, by J. Brandajs; all others by C. Dethier

Chameleon House / All photographs, Anthony Vizzari

Wohnhaus Willimann-Lötscher / All photographs, Bearth & Deplazes Architekten

Salt Point House / All photographs, Scott Frances (Scott Frances.com)

Pine Forest Cabin / All photographs, Art Grice

Glass Shutter House / All photographs, Hiroyuki Hirai

Heran House / All photographs, Bart / Van Leuven / OWI

Modern Wooden Town on the West Bank of Porvoo River / All photographs, Tuomo Siitonen Architects

Laneway House / p. 84 bottom left, Steven Evans; all others by James Dow

Webster Residence / All photographs, Ehrlich Architects

Harless Residence / All photographs, Erhard Pfeiffer

Galley House / p. 102, Steven Evans; all others by Bob Gundu

Option / All photographs, Bauart Architekten und Planer AG

VH R-10 gHouse / All photographs, Bill Timmerman

Slit House / All photographs, Nacasa & Partners

S.H. / All photographs, Kei Sugino

## Townhouses

Kanamori House / All photographs, Tadao Ando Architect & Associates

Townhouse in DC / All photographs, Paul Warchol (Paul Warchol Photography)

Fitch/O'Rourke Residence / pp. 145 bottom left and 147 bottom left, Anice Hoachlander (Hoachlander Davis Photography); all others by Paul Warchol (Paul Warchol Photography)

T Residence / All photographs, Wade Zimmerman

Wohnpark am Betzenberg / All photographs, AV1 Architekten Butz Dujmovic Schanné

Borneo Sporenburg / All photographs, Ger van de Vlugt

Eight Terraced Houses / All photographs, Enrique Mínguez Martínez & Antonio López Sánchez

Slice House / All photographs, Sue Barr (UK) and Marcelo Nunes (BR)

Outeiro House / All photographs, João Ferrand

# INDEX